# HOLYWOOD

*An Illustrated History and Companion*

**Paintings and Drawings**
**by**
**Joanna Martin**

**Text by**
**Tony Merrick**

Cottage

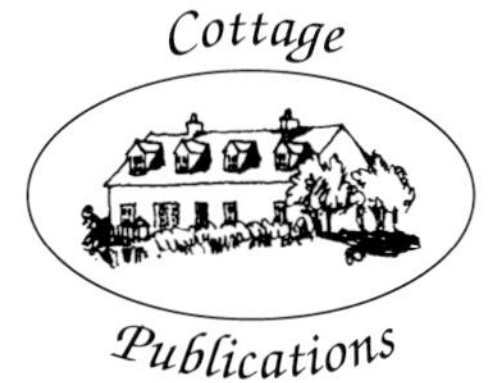

Publications

First published by Cottage Publications,
Donaghadee N. Ireland 1993.

Printed by: Tien Wah Press 977 Bukit
Timah Rd Singapore 2158

ISBN 0 9516402 2 4

# *List of Contents*

# The Artist

Joanna Martin was brought up in Holywood and graduated in Book Illustration and Graphic Design from Edinburgh College of Art in 1984. She then spent some time in London, working full time as a graphic designer for Dorling Kindersley and Country Living Magazine. After a spell with Triplicate Design in Belfast, Joanna established her own business from the Attic Studio in Holywood's Shore Road (see directory).

As well as running a busy graphic design business, Joanna has made time to develop her illustrative skills with recent published work appearing in 'Irish Blessings' (1992), 'Ulster – An Illustrated Yearbook' (1993) and 'The Book of Escapes' (Country Living Magazine 1993).

# The Author

A life long resident of Holywood, Anthony C. W. Merrick has been deeply interested in local history since his teenage years. He is well known in the area for his efforts to promote an awareness of local heritage.

As well as regular contributions to local newspapers he has written a number of books including volumes of gravestone inscriptions for Bangor Abbey (1978), Friar's Bush Graveyard, Belfast (1984) and the New Burying Ground, Belfast (1991). 'Buildings of Holywood' appeared in 1986.

An Architectural technician by occupation, photography and manuscript illumination are among his other interests.

# The Sanctuary by the Sea

The town of Holywood is situated on the County Down shore of Belfast Lough, six miles from Belfast. Attractively positioned against the backdrop of the Holywood hills, most of the district commands a fine view of the Co. Antrim hills on the opposite shore and enjoys the added advantage of being only fifteen minutes travelling time from the centre of Belfast, whether one is using the road or railway. Today the town and its immediate environs boast a population of approximately 14,000 and serves primarily as a dormitory town for Belfast although it has developed its own thriving commercial heart primarily based on the service sector. This was not always the case.

Although there is now nothing above ground level in either Holywood or the surrounding locality dating from earlier than about 1180, flints and axe heads dug up in the Kinnegar sand dunes in the 19th century, have been dated to the early Iron Age (c. 500 B.C.). This discovery seems to indicate the earliest human occupation in the district and the likelihood is that these early predecessors of ours were hunters and fisher-folk, quite possibly attracted by the vast mussel beds which are still in existence, albeit in a somewhat polluted state. Archeological excavations carried out in the late 1950's on the site of a rath near the upper end of Croft Rd, resulted in finds such as bronze pins which were authoritatively dated to between the fifth and seventh centuries of the Christian Era.

The first documentary evidence for human activity at Holywood occurs under the year 642 when the clergy in Rome, in reply to a letter from the leading clergy in the North of Ireland regarding the date of Easter, list a cleric named Laiseran. The Felire of Aengus, a manual of festivals of saints, compiled in the early 9th century, identifies this cleric as St. Laiseran who was "*son of Nasca, of Ard–mac–Nasca* (Gaelic for "height of the son of Nasca" and the original name of Holywood) *on the banks of Lough Laoigh* (Lake of the Calf, nowadays Belfast Lough) *in Ultonia*". As the place was named after him, it is likely that he founded the monastery at Holywood. Nasca was a local princess and it has been suggested that the height which was named after her was near the present day Twisel Bridge, whilst the monastery was most probably at or near the site of the ruins of the old Priory church. A persistent local legend that the locality near the old Priory church was once occupied by Druids lends further weight to the belief that this is the site of the first ecclesiastical community since it is known that the Druids traditionally buried their dead near water and also that it was common for Druidical sites to be Christianised during the late Celtic period (c. 5th to 12th centuries A.D.).

There is no evidence whatever to indicate what form the settlement took but, as with most Hiberno–Celtic monasteries, it is likely to have consisted of a small and plain church surrounded by such ancillary buildings as a scriptorium and beehive shaped huts in which the monks dwelt, all the structures being made of wattle and daub. The whole monastic enclosure would have been surrounded by a wooden palisade within which the local population and livestock could have been gathered in times of danger.

It is almost certain that the community at Holywood would have been ravaged by the Vikings during the raids which they repeatedly carried out on the monastery at Bangor during the 9th century.

In 1177 Sir John de Courcy, an Anglo–Norman adventurer, had invaded Ulster defeating the local King, Rory McDunleevy, and declared himself "Earl of Ulster". About the year 1190 it is recorded that one Thomas Whyte acting as de Courcy's agent re-established the monastic community at Holywood as an Augustinian Abbey, this particular order having been introduced to Ireland from the continent approximately 50 years previously. The new community which was a daughter house of that at Bangor, appears to have replaced the Hiberno–Celtic establishment which had probably been swept away by the Anglo–Normans during their invasion of Ulster. The ruins of the church built at this time survive as the old Priory church which, despite having been altered in the 15th century, still exhibits much of the traditional Romanesque cut stonework.

When de Courcy was disgraced in 1204, his lands in Ulster were confiscated by King John and granted to the de Lacy family. They too attempted to assume autonomous powers, and the authority of the King was only re–established when he invaded Ulster in 1210, capturing Carrickfergus castle. It is on record that he spent the night of 29th July that year "apud Sanctum Boscum", this, translated from the Norman–French, being the first reference to Holywood by its present name. The Norman lands in Ulster then passed to John de Saukvill. Holywood is named in its English form for the first time in 1306 when the taxation roll for the Diocese of Down, Connor and Dromore, compiled on the orders of Pope Nicholas, values the church and its townlands at "Haliwode" at six Marks, this being the equivalent of £4.

The late 14th century saw control of the eastern half of Ulster, then part of the kingdom of Dalriada, gradually wrested from the Anglo–Normans by the native Irish. Following the murder near Skegoneil, in what is nowadays North Belfast, of William de Burgh, Earl of Ulster in 1333, the O'Neill clan launched a series of raids from their base in what is now Co Tyrone and while the O'Neills gained overall control of the area, the Holywood district was apportioned to one of their septs, the O'Gilmores. The Abbey passed to the Third Order of Franciscans about the year 1490 when it was also heavily endowed, certainly with land and probably with money, by the local chieftain Niall O'Neill; at this time the church was extensively remodelled.

Throughout the mediaeval period it is likely that a small township clustered in the area between the monastic graveyard, the Motte and the river Twisel to the west but there is no archeological evidence of such occupation.

The 16th century was a period of decline and destruction for the province of Ulster. The priory (as it had now become) was officially dissolved on 1st January 1541 by the agents of King Henry VIII, the last prior being Connor O'Hamill and its possessions which included the townlands of Ballykeel, Ballymenoch, Ballycultra, Ballyknocknagoney and Ballyderry were by law vested in the Crown, although in practice the local chieftains still held sway. It is quite possible that the church continued to be used for divine service until it was burnt in October 1572 by the local chieftain, Sir Brian MacPhelim O'Neill in an effort to deny shelter to the troops of Sir Thomas Smith who was engaged in a futile attempt to colonise Ulster on behalf of Queen Elizabeth I. It is likely that the conventual buildings of the monastic establishment would have finally disappeared at this time together with any nearby settlement.

The modern town of Holywood can justifiably be said to have been founded in the very early 17th century. Towards the end of the reign of Elizabeth I, close friends and favourites of James VI of Scotland (soon to be James I of England) had been casting covetous eyes towards Ulster which increasingly looked as though it would become easy prey as the power of the Irish chieftains was by now fast crumbling. When the plantation settlement finally began in the first decade of the new century, the Clannaboy district, comprising what is now North Down and part of South Antrim, was granted by the King to Sir James Hamilton and James Montgomery, only one third of the original land being retained by Sir Con O'Neill, the last local Irish chieftain.

Hamilton, an adventurer from near Dunlop in Ayrshire, received that tract of land stretching from near Donaghadee to Castlereagh. Ruthless and resourceful, he proceeded to reconstitute both Bangor and Holywood as market towns and rebuilt both monastic churches for parish church use. Holywood acquired its present basic cruciform street plan about the year 1615, and Thomas Raven's street map of 1625 clearly shows a small maypole in approximately the position occupied by the present one. Quite plainly the dwellings were all single storied and thatched.

The Raven map shows the stretch of High St between the maypole and the old Priory church as being wider than the remainder of the street, a layout which still survives as a reminder of the market established under the terms of the original patent, granted to Sir James Hamilton on 5th November 1606, stipulating that it was to be held every Wednesday and an annual fair on 24th March (at that time New Year's Eve). It flourished through the 17th century, only to finally peter out about the year 1840.

The 1641 rebellion and the subsequent Civil War brought tragedy and disgrace to the district for in January 1642 seventy three members of the Gilmore sept in Ballydavey townland, near Craigavad, were massacred by planters from both Holywood and Bangor. Cromwellian soldiers are reputed to have come to the village in 1654. The Williamite Wars only touched on the life of Holywood in that the army of the Duke of Schomberg encamped on Standard Hill about one mile to the south east, whilst on the march from Groomsport to the Boyne in 1690.

Holywood and the surrounding area was owned by the Hamilton family for generations until, in order to settle inherited debts in the family, it became necessary to sell parts of the estate. An early casualty was that portion of the estate encompassing Cultra, Craigavad and Ballyrobert which was acquired by the Kennedys, an aristocratic Scottish family, in 1668.

In 1705 Hans Hamilton sold the townland of Holywood, 725 acres in extent and taking in most of the village; he also sold the Priory House and gardens and that part of the townland of Ballykeel immediately surrounding the old Priory church and later called Priory Park, to their agent, Simon Isaac from Ballywalter, for the sum of £1,150. The manorial rights were acquired by the Hill family, which was subsequently ennobled as Viscount Dungannon. In 1765 Simon Isaac, grandson of the first Simon, added Knocknagoney townland so doubling the size of the estate. It was also he who built Holywood House.

The entire estate was sold by the Isaac family in 1812 to one William Kennedy, a merchant who had built up his fortune in India, for £38,000; he was unrelated to the family of the same name of Cultra. In 1854, representatives of the Kennedy family sold the estates to John Harrison, a shipping agent and merchant of Belfast and living at Mertoun Hall; within a comparatively short time the Holywood estate was broken up.

A similar fate befell portions of the Kennedy estate and in the late 18th century other propertied families erected large mansions, colloquially known as "Big Houses", in the district. These included the Turnleys of Richmond Lodge at Knocknagoney and Rockport House, the Holmes and later the Gregs of Ballymenoch House, and in 1827 the Bishop of Down, Connor and Dromore built the Bishops Palace at the site of the modern Palace Barracks.

Throughout the 17th and 18th centuries Holywood had remained essentially a small thatched village containing three or four hundred inhabitants whose principal occupations were weaving and fishing. The extensive banks of mussels off the Kinnegar provided much of the staple diet (supplemented with potatoes and oatmeal) of the poorer people who, as we are told by the noted historian Walter Harris when writing of the village in his County Down Survey in 1744, made their fare more exciting by the addition of butter, pepper and onions. The reminiscences of old people, recorded in 1870, state that it was quite usual to see bluish–black piles of mussel shells outside cottages in High St with patches of grass growing in between on which fowl fed, there being no proper footpath. Even as late as the year 1800 the village, which extended from the old Priory church to the site of the modern junction of Downshire Rd with High St, boasted only three slated houses and these were two storeys high. During this period the people of Holywood were almost exclusively Presbyterian (both Subscribing and non–Subscribing), a census taken in 1764 also informing us that the population of the entire parish which then stretched from the River Connswater in present day East Belfast to Gray Point, stood at nearly 1,800.

The coming of the 19th century saw comparatively peaceful conditions return to the country in general, and also a new fashion for sea bathing. This latter development was to prove particularly significant for Holywood, for this led to a sudden and rapid realisation of its potential as both a health resort and a dormitory town for the merchants of Belfast, particularly attractive aspects being the bracing climate and clean beaches, combined with the proximity of Belfast. The first real step came in 1810 when the village received its first two coach services, one run by John Rowley of the Strand area of Holywood which plied between Ann St Belfast and his own house, and the other by Daniel Miskelly of North St Belfast. The first Post Office opened in 1818, Hugh Stewart who soon rose to prominence as one of Holywood's leading citizens and property owners, being appointed Post Master in 1822. He was also responsible for starting the resort's first public baths, a rather short lived venture, in the

Strand district in 1824. The Rev. W.A. Holmes, Vicar of Holywood, in his statistical survey of the parish completed in 1817, stated that many of the residents supported themselves by letting their dwellings to visitors during the summer. Many of those who came initially as weekend and summer visitors liked Holywood so much that they subsequently bought either the cottages or vacant plots and made the place their permanent home. By this time fishing was a fast dying industry and it is recorded that by 1844 only 14 fishermen remained.

The Ordinance Survey memoirs of 1834 describe the village as "a pleasurable summer residence, especially for those who are daily obliged to be in Belfast". The thirty years between 1810 and 1841 saw Holywood radically transformed from a fishing community of a few hundred, living in rude thatched cabins, to a flourishing seaside resort of 1,532 people living in 263 dwellings. During that time it acquired a constabulary police station manned by a sergeant and a constable, a sessions house (mostly for civil cases), a house of industry, a coastguard station and a dispensary. The 1834 survey of the village indicates that well over half of the dwellings were now slated. Between 1841 and 1865 the population doubled and the work of rebuilding was essentially completed. In January 1865 the town boundaries were greatly extended to encompass this growth.

This sudden burgeoning was due to the influx of Belfast merchants who were experiencing an unprecedented boom in prosperity resulting from the industrial revolution in the early 19th century which also led to the meteoric growth of that town. No longer were they content to "live over the shop" in the noisy, cramped and often insanitary conditions of High St and Ann St as they had done for two centuries. Now their newly found wealth, together with improved transport, offered both the incentive and opportunity to take up their abode in more salubrious and healthy surroundings such as the Malone ridge to the south of Belfast, Whitehouse and Holywood; thus the commuter age was born.

The process was accelerated by the opening in 1848 of the Belfast to Holywood railway, the easy access from Belfast paving the way for a broader cross–section of the populace. Among the merchants who came at this period and erected elegant mansions was Jonathan Cordukes, a prosperous provisions merchant and town councillor from York St Belfast and soon to be prominent in the affairs of Holywood, who arrived in 1832. He was followed soon afterwards by John Heron, one of the co–founders of the Ulster Bank, who bought Maryfield, the site of which is nowadays occupied by the offices of the Anglo–Irish Secretariat. Other "merchant princes" arrived to grace the slopes at the back of the town, later known as High Holywood, with their palaces commanding unrivalled views of Belfast Lough. These included Henry Murney, a leading tobacco merchant from High St in Belfast, who built Tudor House near the Bangor Rd in 1849 and Foster Green the prominent Belfast tea merchant who was responsible for Marmion near Church Rd in the late 1850's. Bernard ("Barney") Hughes, founder of the famous bakery, bought Riverston House, beside the old Motte, in 1869, whilst the Read brothers, founders of the "Belfast Morning News" lived nearby. Millbank, also on the Victoria Rd, was built almost on the exact site of a water powered mill. The Dunville family, of whiskey fame, built Redburn House in the late 1860's.

Not only did the mercantile classes settle in Holywood but academics from the newly opened Queen's College in Belfast (now University) found the tranquil and convenient surroundings conducive to study and there were also plenty of artisans such as plumbers, carpenters, builders and blacksmiths residing in the area. The town's growing reputation as a place of retirement and a spa for invalids necessarily brought in its wake those of the medical profession. James D. Marshall, the well known Belfast apothecary and son of one of the founders of the profession there, came to live in Shore St (nowadays Rd). John Gabbey practised as a surgeon at 88 High St and in the early 1870's John Charles Payne of Shaftesbury Sq. in Belfast, founded the medical hall which was ultimately to become Sweeney's Pharmacies Ltd. Dr Archibald Dunlop who built St. Helen's in High St in 1876 and was a benefactor of the Parish church, was the town's medical officer from 1857 until 1902.

Holywood's role as a watering place gave rise to the holiday homes and boarding houses which sprang up in Marine Parade, the lower part of Shore St and the Strand area (the development of the Kinnegar area did not get under way until the 1860's). There was no shortage of hotels, the best known being the Belfast Hotel in High St, nowadays the Lynch Building, and the Marine Hotel in Marine Parade. The institution which proved to be the biggest attraction was the salt water baths opened by the Holywood Baths Company at the bottom of Shore St in 1852, providing both hot and cold, salt and fresh water baths.

Such was the pace of development that Holywood was raised to the dignity of a town and Town Commissioners were established in January 1852, a form of local government that was to remain until 1899 when the Holywood Urban District Council was set up. They provided such public amenities as sewage disposal and the supply of water. It was only natural that the expanding community's new found status should be reflected in some buildings of architectural distinction.

The Presbyterians replaced their small meeting house in the Strand area with a rather handsome Gothic style church on the Bangor Rd, designed by their own minister, the Rev. William Blackwood, in 1841. Three years later the Church of Ireland followed suit when they abandoned the old Priory church in favour of a new place of worship on a site at Church Rd, beyond what was then the edge of the town. It was one of a series at the time being designed for the Diocese by the youthful Charles Lanyon, soon to become the leading Ulster architect of his generation. Lanyon was also responsible for the new Non Subscribing Presbyterian church in High St in 1849, the ornate Sullivan School, founded in 1862 to meet the town's growing educational needs and later in the same decade, the extension of the Parish church. St. Colmcille's beautiful French–Gothic style church by Timothy Hevey, a leading ecclesiastical architect in this country, was consecrated in 1874 on a site also at the edge of the town; sadly it was destroyed by fire in 1989. William Batt, an equally competent architect, was to give Holywood a fine Town Hall in Sullivan Place in 1876.

The one builder to whom the credit must go for the construction of many of the houses and other buildings required to meet this growth was William Nimick (1819–1906) who was responsible for many of the more important edifices of Holywood during the second half of the century.

The growth of the built environment reflected development in social and commercial spheres. In the late 1840's, the Holywood Loan Fund, essentially a private bank, was established in a small building in what is now Downshire Rd. What is now the Holywood Library was heralded in the mid Victorian era by such groups as the Holywood Literary and Scientific Society and a succession of working men's reading rooms, mostly instigated by the various churches. There was also an active Dispensary Committee and Destitute Sick Society, both managed by leading residents. In addition to the three National Schools, basic educational needs were catered for by a host of small private academies, often known as "dame schools", usually accommodated in the homes of the proprietors.

⁂ ⁂ ⁂ ⁂

It was in the 1870's that Holywood's heyday and potential for further expansion as a noted watering resort waned as meteorically as it had arisen half a century previously. This was due entirely to the fact that in 1865 the railway was extended to Bangor, so placing the latter town with its even more attractive amenities, within easy reach of Belfast. In addition, the construction work entailed the formation of a high embankment which separated the town of Holywood from the sea, so rendering the shore difficult of access; this was the height of irony considering that Holywood owed its most rapid period of growth to the arrival of the railway seventeen years beforehand. For the last 30 years of the Victorian era its population remained fairly constant at 3,500. Correspondingly, there were few major building works in the last twenty years of the century.

There was a resurgence of growth in the early years of the 20th century, which was characterised by the erection by the business and professional sections of the community of suburban type houses. The years since the second world war have seen the town rapidly expand well beyond the limits defined about a century before, largely because of the widely based prosperity associated with the 'fifties and 'sixties. The most notable developments in the early part of the post war boom were the Loughview and Redburn housing estates built by the N.I. Housing Trust in 1948 and 1956 respectively; parallel with the public sector, the Princess Gardens estate off the Croft Rd was privately built in 1948. Large swathes of the old part of the town disappeared with the total rebuilding of the Hill St area by the Holywood Urban District Council in 1965, and from 1967 to 1971 the Strand area was completely redeveloped by the Housing Trust. The late 'sixties saw the very large Braemere Heights estate erected by a private developer at Marino to the east of the town.

The 'seventies and 'eighties was a time of continued provision of private estates for the executive and professional clientele in Princess Gardens and the Ardmore district off the Croft Rd. An additional phenomenon of this period has been an upsurge of "infill" dwellings in the gardens of the larger and older properties. The Holywood of today has essentially retained the character of an early Victorian town for almost overnight at the turn of the century it became little more than a pleasant backwater, serving as a dormitory town for Belfast merchants and businessmen.

With the nationwide redistribution of the local councils in 1973, the Holywood Urban District Council, which had served the community well for three–quarters of a century, was wound up, and the town has since been administered by the North Down Borough Council which has worked with the Holywood Residents Association and the Holywood Community Council in looking after local interests. In 1992 Holywood won the "Best Kept Large Town" award and in 1993 civic pride was further enhanced when the former Sullivan School building was opened for use as the Holywood Library.

T.M.
1993.

# The Growth of Holywood

| Year | Population |
|---|---|
| 1841 | 1,532 |
| 1861 | 2,442 |
| 1901 | 3,840 |
| 1947 | 6,345 |
| 1991 | 14,200 |

# Main Events in Holywood's History

c. 500 B.C. Early Iron Age settlers living in the Kinnegar area .

4-500 A.D. Rath type settlement near the upper reaches of present day Croft Rd.

c. 640 Monastery founded by St Laiseran, almost certainly on site of old Priory church.

c. 1190 Thomas Whyte, acting for John de Courcy, Earl of Ulster, refounded monastery as an Augustinian Abbey.

1210 King John spends one night at Holywood in July during his campaign to restore his authority over Ulster.

13–1400 Anglo–Norman power in the area collapses. Holywood district under sway of O'Gilmore sept.

c.1490 Abbey at Holywood becomes Franciscan, yet remains a daughter house of Bangor which was Augustinian.

1541 Priory formally dissolved during Dissolution of Monasteries. Last Prior was Connor O'Hamill.

1572 Priory church at Holywood burned by Sir Brian MacPhelim O'Neill during fighting with English forces.

1606–15 Lands of North Down, including Holywood, granted to Sir James Hamilton by King James I.

1615 First Presbyterian congregation founded.

1642 Massacre of O'Gilmores at Ballydavey townland.

c.1800–10 Holywood changes from fishing village to bathing and health resort.

1810 First regular coach services to Belfast provided.

1824 First baths established.

| | |
|---|---|
| **c.1815–30** | Holywood acquired such establishments as Post Office, Dispensary, House of Industry, Constabulary Station, Sessions House and a Coastguard Station. |
| **1834** | Replacement of thatched cottages with slated houses well underway. |
| **1848** | Belfast and Holywood railway opened. |
| **1852** | Holywood officially became a town. Holywood Baths Company opened fresh and salt water baths. |
| **1860** | Holywood Gasworks opened. |
| **1865** | Official town boundaries greatly extended. The railway line was extended to Bangor. |
| **1866** | Town provided with piped sewage system. |
| **1898** | Holywood Urban District Council replaced Town Commissioners. |
| **c. 1900** | Holywood embarked on a further period of expansion. |
| **1948–49** | 400 dwellings provided at Loughview by N.I Housing Trust to accommodate both people from the older parts of Holywood and people from the York Rd area of Belfast who lost their homes during the Blitz. |
| **1953** | Queens Hall opened as replacement for old Town Hall. |
| **1967–71** | Redevelopment of Strand area of Holywood. |
| **1973** | Holywood Urban District Council wound up and administrative functions transferred to newly formed North Down Borough Council. |
| **1983** | Regular May–Day celebrations re–instituted. |
| **1992** | Holywood wins "Best Kept Large Town" award for Northern Ireland. |
| **1993** | Old Sullivan School building re–opened as Holywood library. |

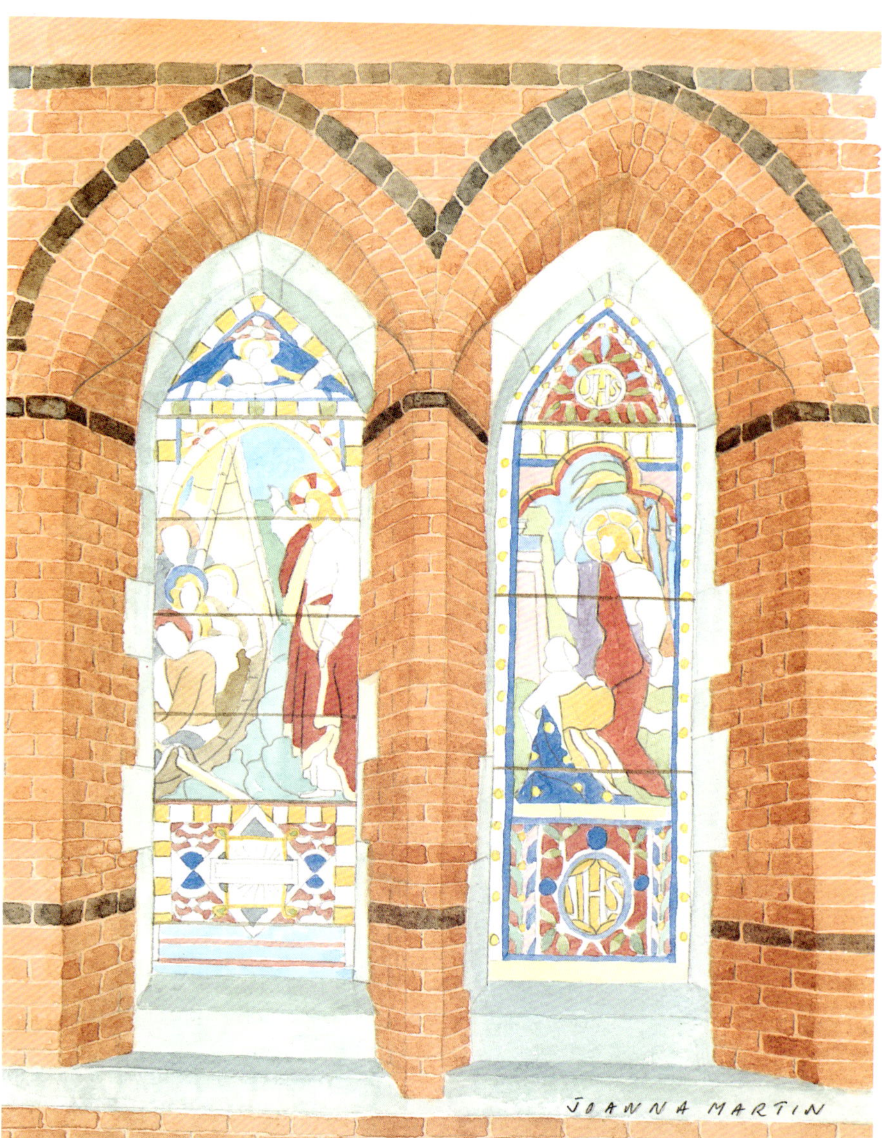
JOANNA MARTIN

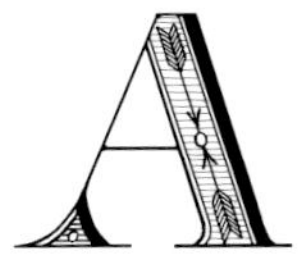

| *Name and Address* | *Telephone* |
|---|---|
| | |
| | |
| | |
| | |
| | |
| | |
| | |
| | |
| | |
| | |
| | |
| | |
| | |

**PARISH CHURCH OF SS PHILIP AND JAMES.**

During the thirty or so years following the construction in 1869 of the present nave, chancel and north aisle, the windows of the church were beautified by the insertion of stained glass. This charming pair of small lancet windows is located in the Manning Memorial Chapel in the north aisle. The left hand window shows Our Lord walking on the water and commemorates Sir Arthur Edward Kennedy (1810–1883) of Cultra, a Governor of Queensland. He was also an uncle of Sir Robert Kennedy, the noted diplomat. The theme of the right hand window is the raising of Lazarus and is in memory of Sir Arthur's wife who died in 1874.

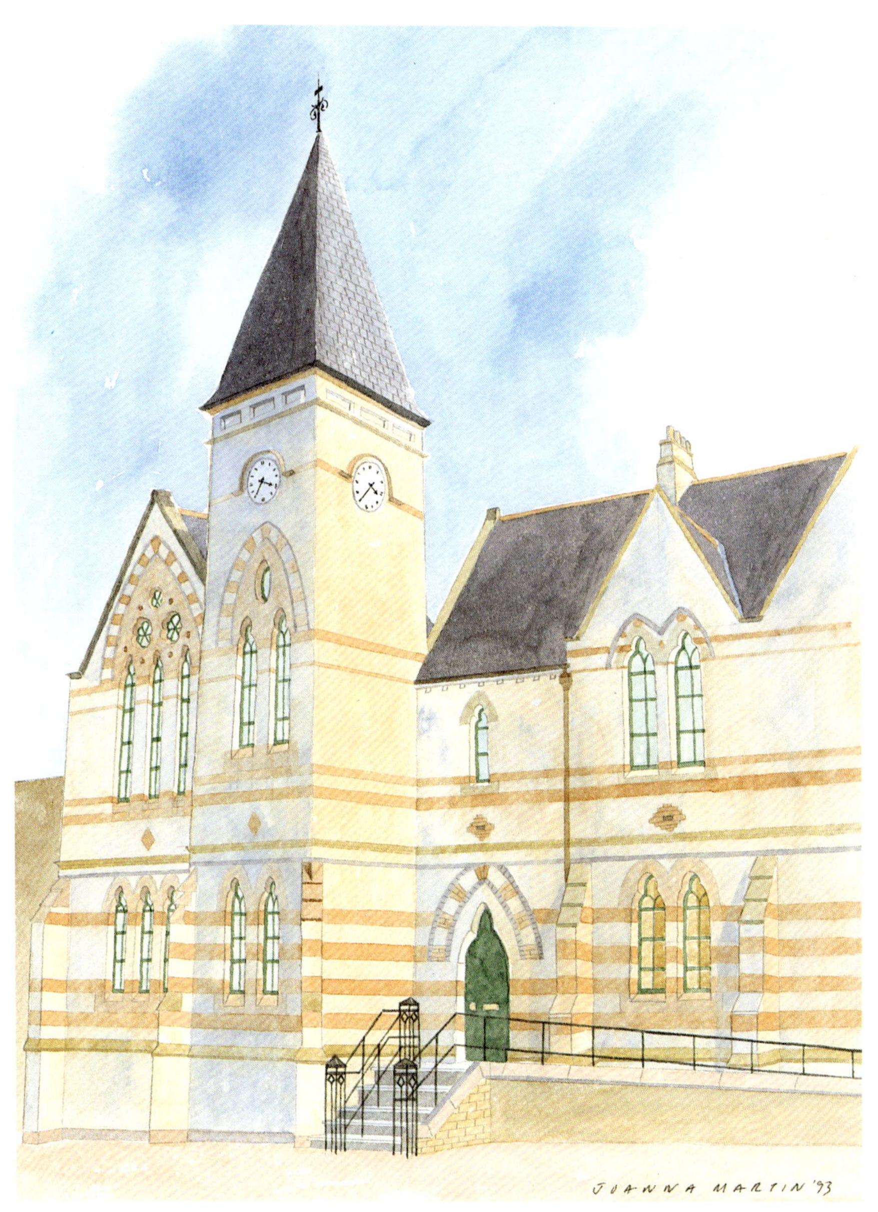
JOANNA MARTIN '93

# B

| *Name and Address* | *Telephone* |
| --- | --- |
| | |
| | |
| | |
| | |
| | |
| | |
| | |
| | |
| | |
| | |
| | |
| | |
| | |

**HOLYWOOD LIBRARY, SULLIVAN BUILDING, HIGH STREET.**

This building was originally constructed in two stages, the entire cost of £4,000 being borne by the noted educationalist Dr Robert Sullivan (1800 – 1868) who was born and bred locally. The first portion to the right was completed in 1862 as the Holywood National School for younger children. To house older pupils a second phase of building, including the distinctive clock tower, was added in 1877, the two parts becoming known as the Lower and Upper Sullivan Schools respectively. The building currently houses the Holywood Library, officially opened in April 1993. From whichever angle it is viewed, it is integral to the streetscape of the town's main thoroughfare.

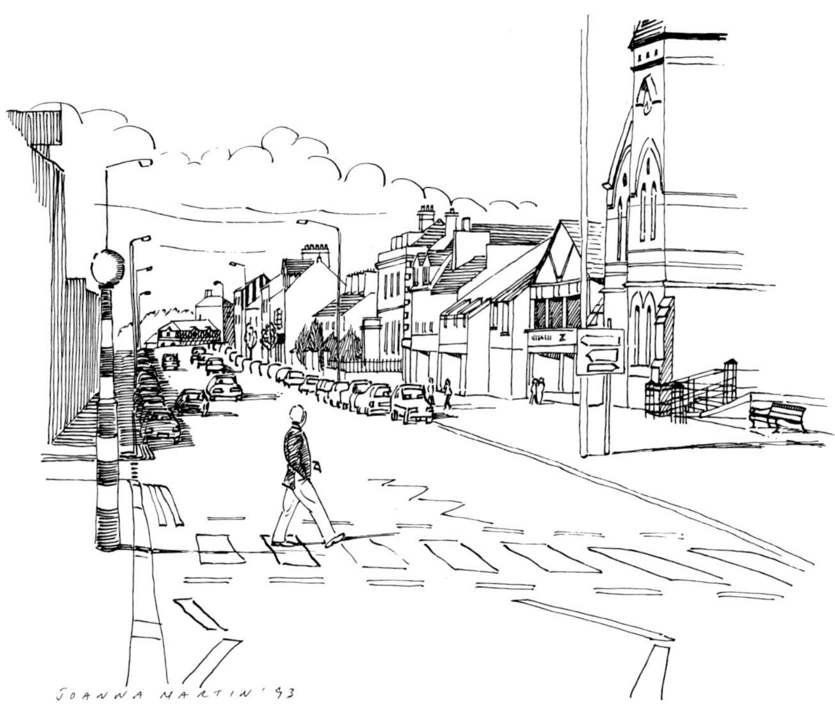
JOANNA MARTIN '93

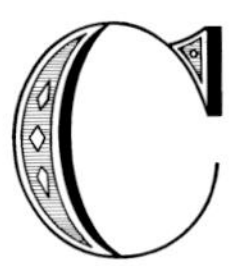

| *Name and Address* | *Telephone* |
|---|---|
| | |
| | |
| | |
| | |
| | |
| | |
| | |
| | |
| | |
| | |
| | |
| | |
| | |

HIGH STREET.

This is one of Holywood's original streets and until the construction of the through-pass in 1972, lay on the main Belfast to Bangor Road. Raven's map of 1625 shows it to have been built up to about half its present length, but the overall form remains the same. This view, looking towards the maypole from the corner with Sullivan Place, shows a broad spectrum of commercial premises and some cottage style houses which are still inhabited, ranging in date from the 1830's to the 1980's. Part of the old Sullivan Schools is visible on the extreme right.

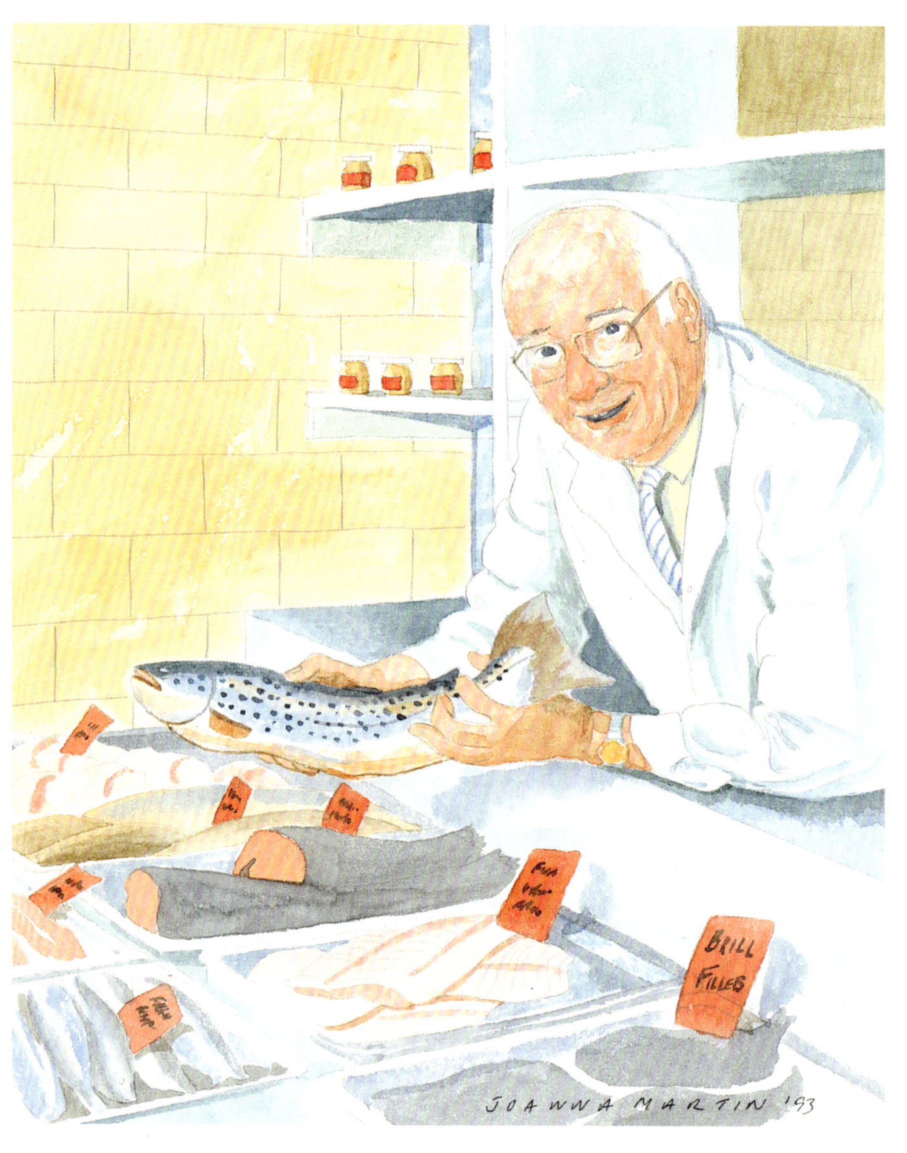
BRILL FILLETS
JOANNA MARTIN '93

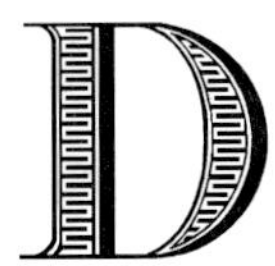

| *Name and Address* | *Telephone* |
|---|---|
| | |
| | |
| | |
| | |
| | |
| | |
| | |
| | |
| | |
| | |
| | |
| | |
| | |

**FISHMONGER'S SHOP, 64 HIGH STREET.**

These premises were built as a shop with the usual living accommodation upstairs during the 1870's. Among a number of well known occupants of this shop were Mr and Mrs McCreedy who ran a confectionery shop and ice-cream parlour from 1901 until the 1930's. They were followed by Fred Balmer who was a provision merchant and fishmonger until about 1960. When Mr Ivan James, the present owner, succeeded him, he concentrated on selling fish. The shop has kept many of its original fittings. Its marble counter and shelves, tiled walls and floor retain much of the look it had in the 1930's. Interestingly this was the first shop in Holywood to install electricity.

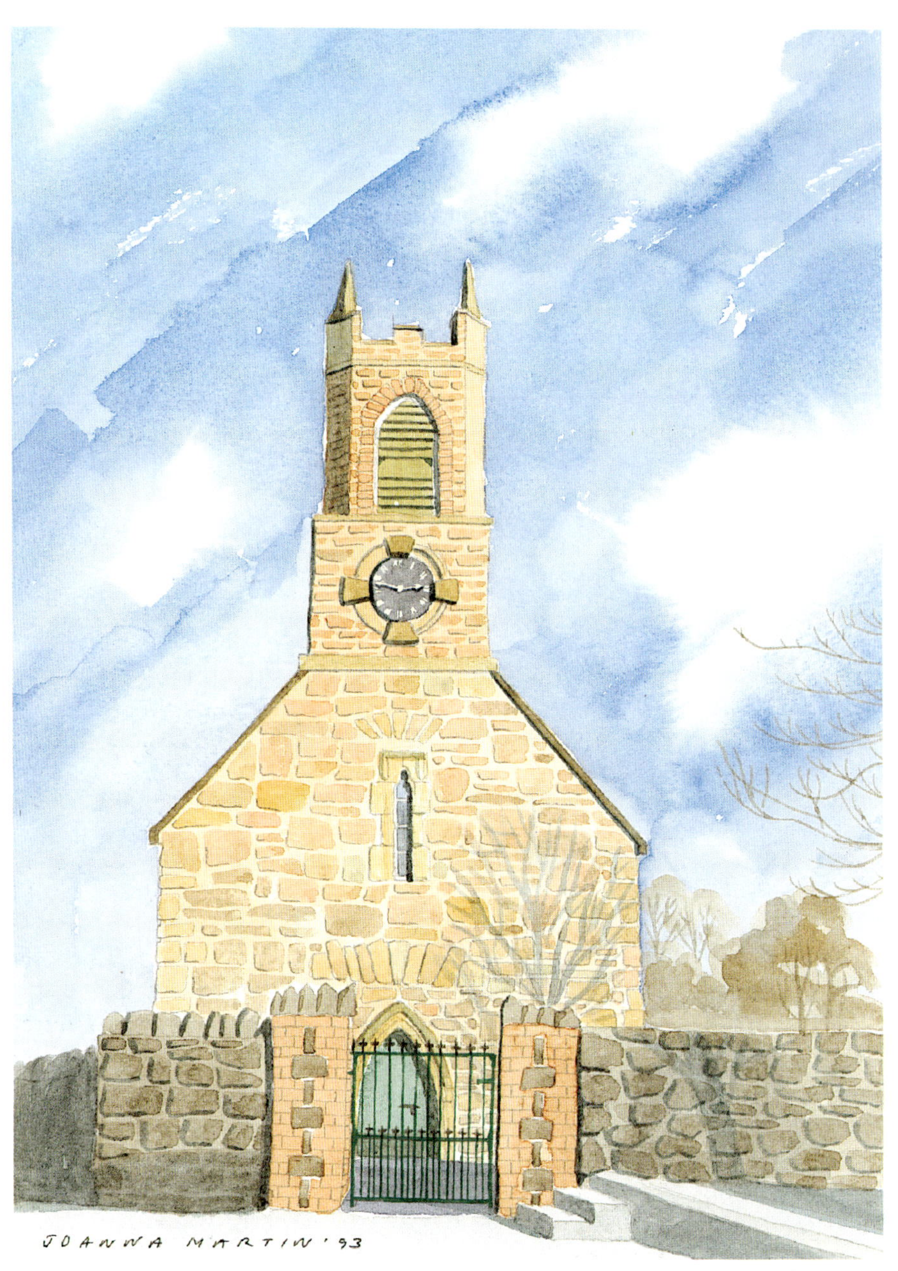
JOANNA MARTIN '93

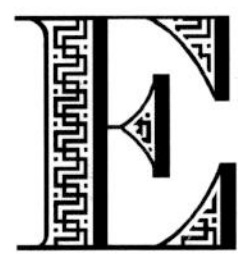

| *Name and Address* | *Telephone* |
| --- | --- |
| | |
| | |
| | |
| | |
| | |
| | |
| | |
| | |
| | |
| | |
| | |
| | |
| | |

**THE OLD PRIORY CHURCH.**

This rather small and simple rectangular structure is essentially the late twelfth century Augustinian Abbey built at the behest of John de Courcy. When it became a Franciscan Priory in about 1490, the east window and the door at the west end were inserted. Further changes occurred when it became the Parish church for both Anglicans and Presbyterians in about 1615 and the quaint-looking octagonal clock tower was added in 1800. Used solely by the Anglicans from 1661, is was finally abandoned as a place of worship in 1844 and was unroofed the following year. The surrounding graveyard is still in use.

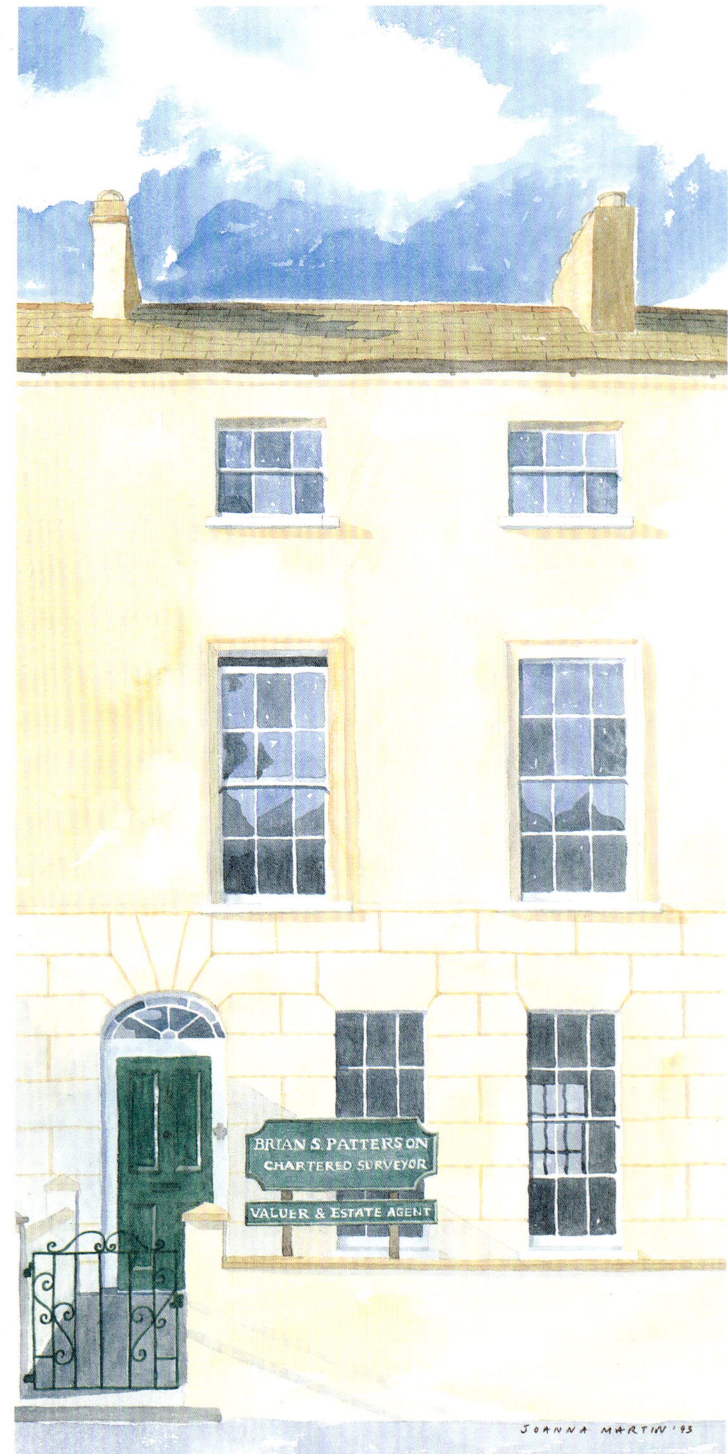
BRIAN S. PATTERSON
CHARTERED SURVEYOR
VALUER & ESTATE AGENT
JOANNA MARTIN '93

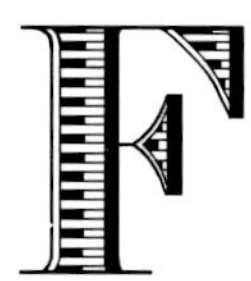

| *Name and Address* | *Telephone* |
|---|---|
| | |
| | |
| | |
| | |
| | |
| | |
| | |
| | |
| | |
| | |
| | |
| | |
| | |

## Shore Road Terrace.

In the late 1820's Shore Street (nowadays Road) was one of those areas of Holywood where the small thatched cottages of the previous century were being replaced with neat and substantial dwellings during the village's transformation from a fishing community to a seaside resort. Although Shore Rd was one of the thoroughfares that had a preponderance of boarding houses and holiday homes, this particular house was originally occupied by a doctor. It is one of a terrace of four which have deep front gardens. It has recently been sympathetically converted to office use for Brian Patterson & Co, Surveyors and Valuers, whilst successfully retaining its architectural character.

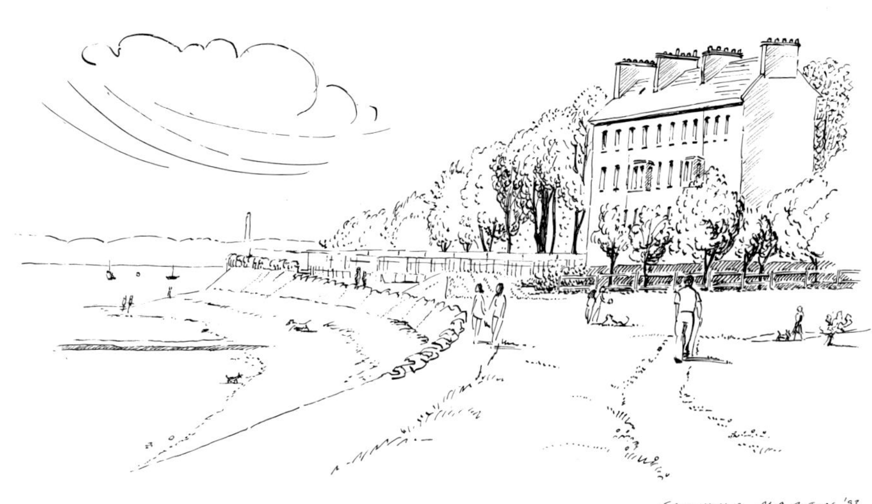
JOANNA MARTIN '93

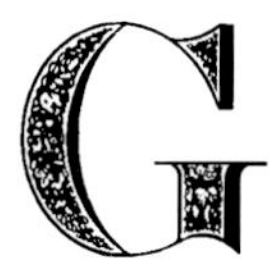

| *Name and Address* | *Telephone* |
|---|---|
| | |
| | |
| | |
| | |
| | |
| | |
| | |
| | |
| | |
| | |
| | |
| | |
| | |

## Clanbrassil Terrace, Cultra.

This view shows three very imposing stucco-faced terrace houses, a type more often found in a select urban setting rather than this position overlooking the North Down Coastal Path. They were erected between 1867 and 1870 by James Connor, a speculative builder and engineer from Belfast, as the beginning of what was to be an exceptionally long terrace stretching over a quarter of a mile to the pier at Cultra. These houses were to cater for the professional people who were then starting to settle in the area. The scheme was curtailed due to a shortage of funds after only four houses were built. The fourth house sited at the west end was burned down soon after being built.

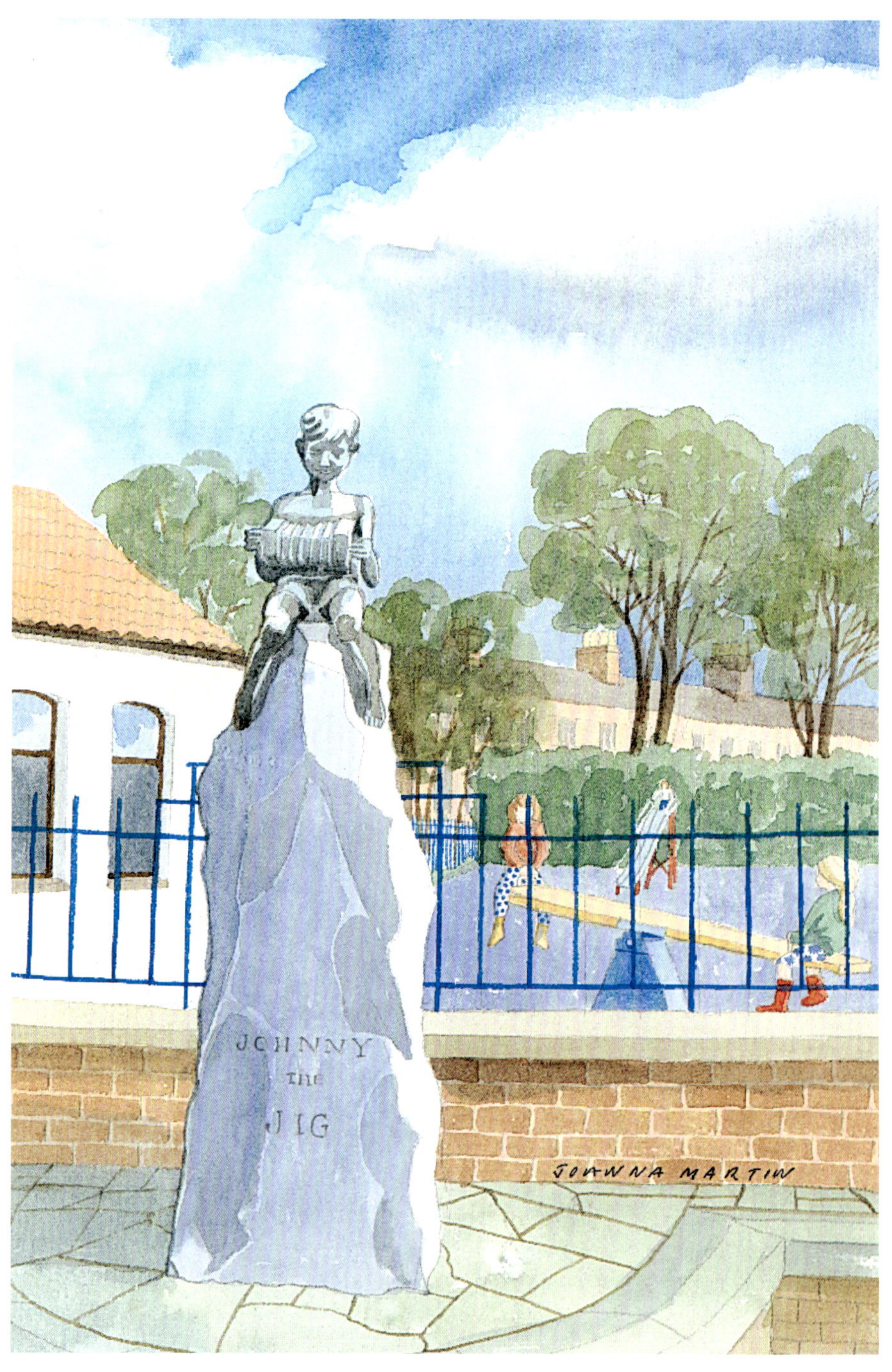
JOHNNY
THE
JIG
JOANNA MARTIN

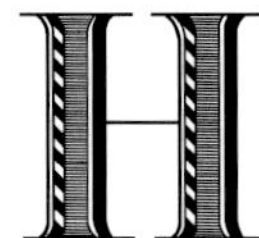

| *Name and Address* | *Telephone* |
|---|---|
| | |
| | |
| | |
| | |
| | |
| | |
| | |
| | |
| | |
| | |
| | |
| | |
| | |

## Johnny the Jig, High Street.

In January 1953 the Praeger Memorial Committee was set up, in the last years of her life, to commemorate the work of the well known local sculptress Rosamund Praeger (1867–1954). It was decided to raise £300 for a bronze casting of a study in plaster of a child playing the accordion, which she had executed in about 1944. It is thought to be an amalgam of three different children including a girl. The name and theme are probably Miss Praeger's inspiration as she was fond of children. The granite base is by Morris Harding, the noted sculptor and the committee chairman. Unveiled in 1953, it is appropriately sited beside a children's playground which was paid for by a friend of Miss Praeger.

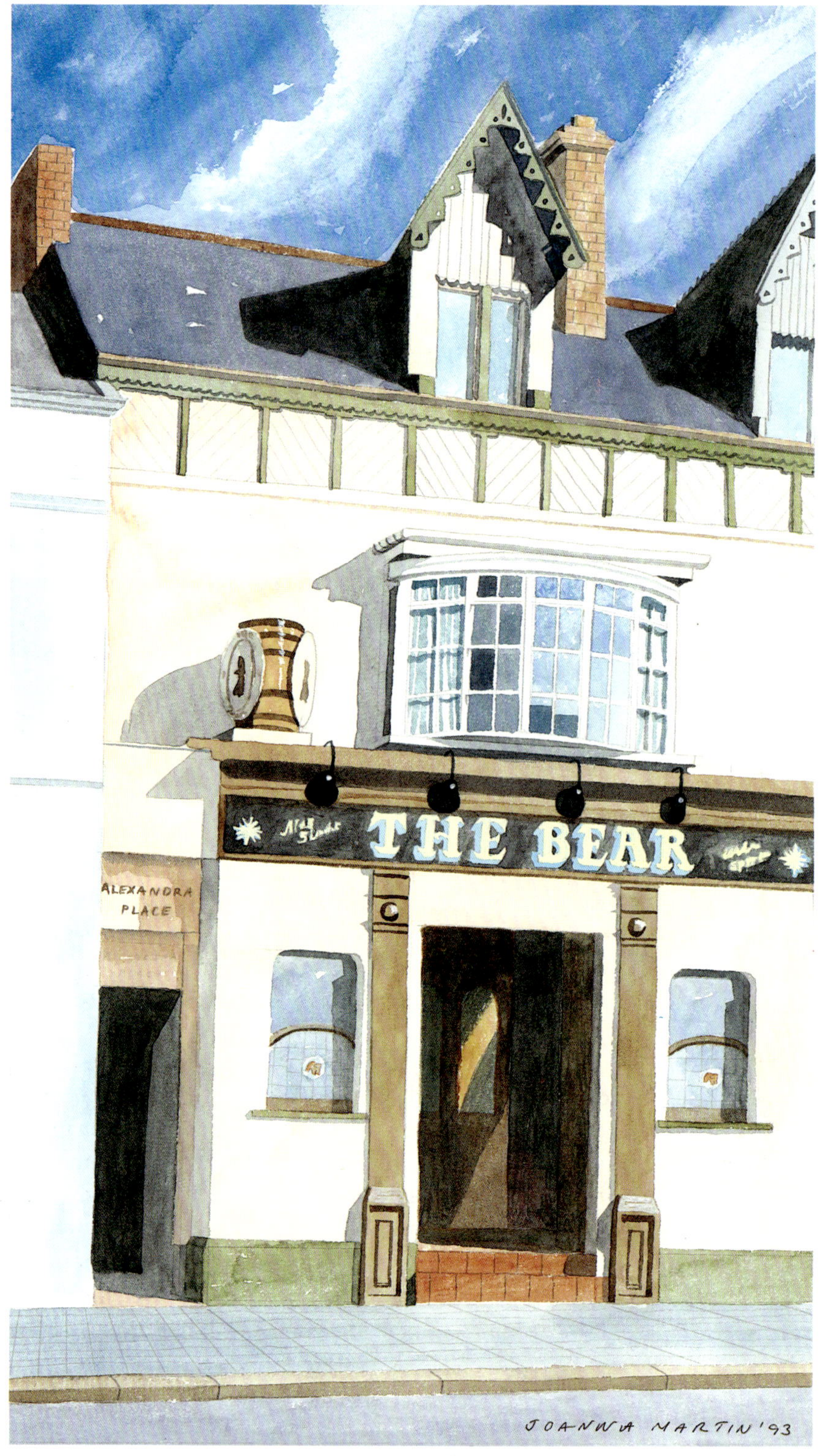
THE BEAR
ALEXANDRA PLACE
JOANNA MARTIN '93

# I

| *Name and Address* | *Telephone* |
| --- | --- |
| | |
| | |
| | |
| | |
| | |
| | |
| | |
| | |
| | |
| | |
| | |
| | |
| | |

**"The Bear", 62 High Street.**

This was built in the 1870's as the "Star Inn" by George McCann, a "dealer" turned publican. Following his death, the business was carried on by his widow until 1898 when it was acquired by Michael Trainor who renamed it the "White Star Inn" and was a well known publican here for many years. Over the last 30 years its facade has undergone several changes, during which time it has been variously named the "Iona", the "Holywood Bowl", the "Gallery" and since 1989 the "Bear" when it was given tasteful Victorian style fittings by its present owner Mr Gerry Reid.

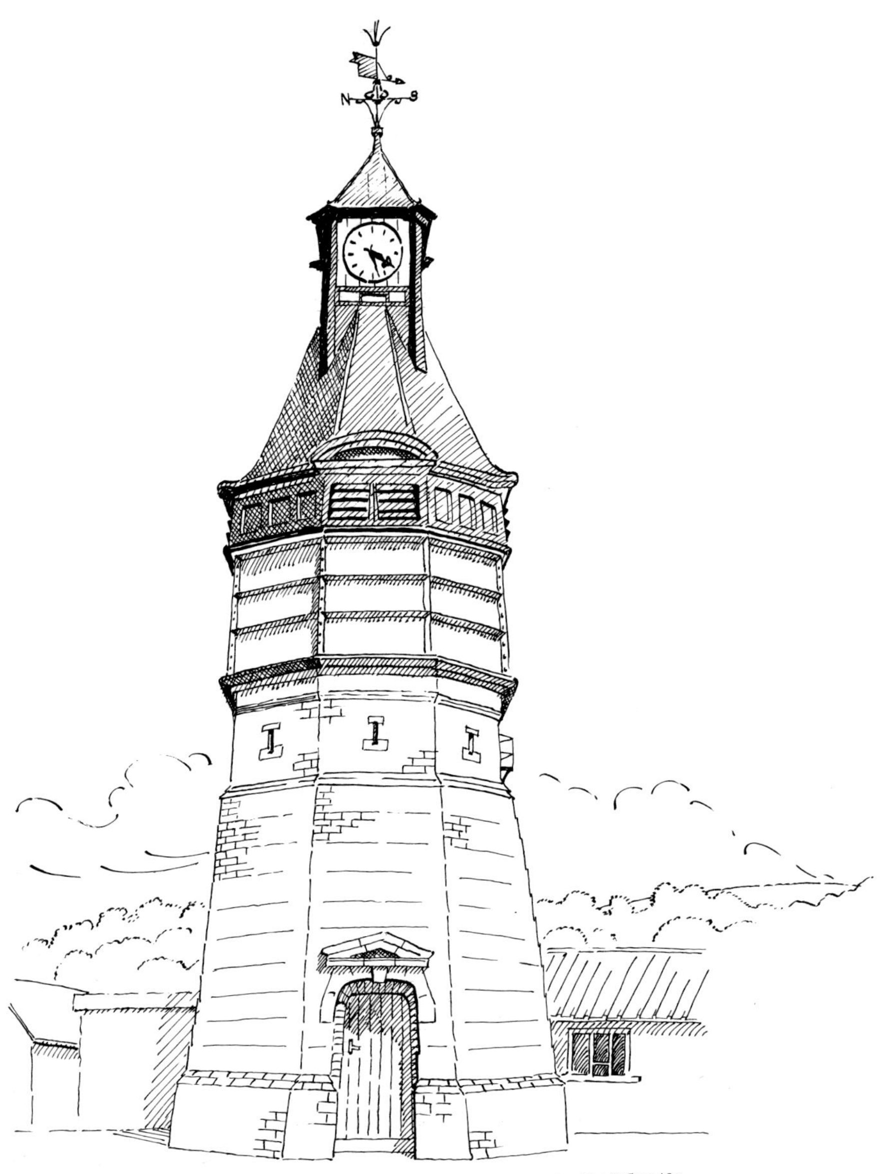
N
S
JOANNA MARTIN '93

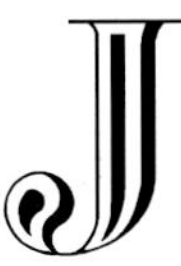

| *Name and Address* | *Telephone* |
|---|---|
| | |
| | |
| | |
| | |
| | |
| | |
| | |
| | |
| | |
| | |
| | |
| | |
| | |

**CLOCK TOWER, PALACE BARRACKS.**

Holywood's period as a garrison town began in 1885 when several regiments based in Belfast had a summer camp for two months at the western end of the Kinnegar area. This was repeated with even greater numbers over the next few years and in 1887 the War Office bought the old disused, though elegant, Bishop's Palace and its 67 acres. The Palace was demolished in 1890, and on its site the very prominent clock tower was erected in 1899, the architect being Vincent Craig. The soldiers' accommodation blocks and grandiose Officers' Mess nearby were built at the same time, so creating one of the largest military barracks in Ireland at that period.

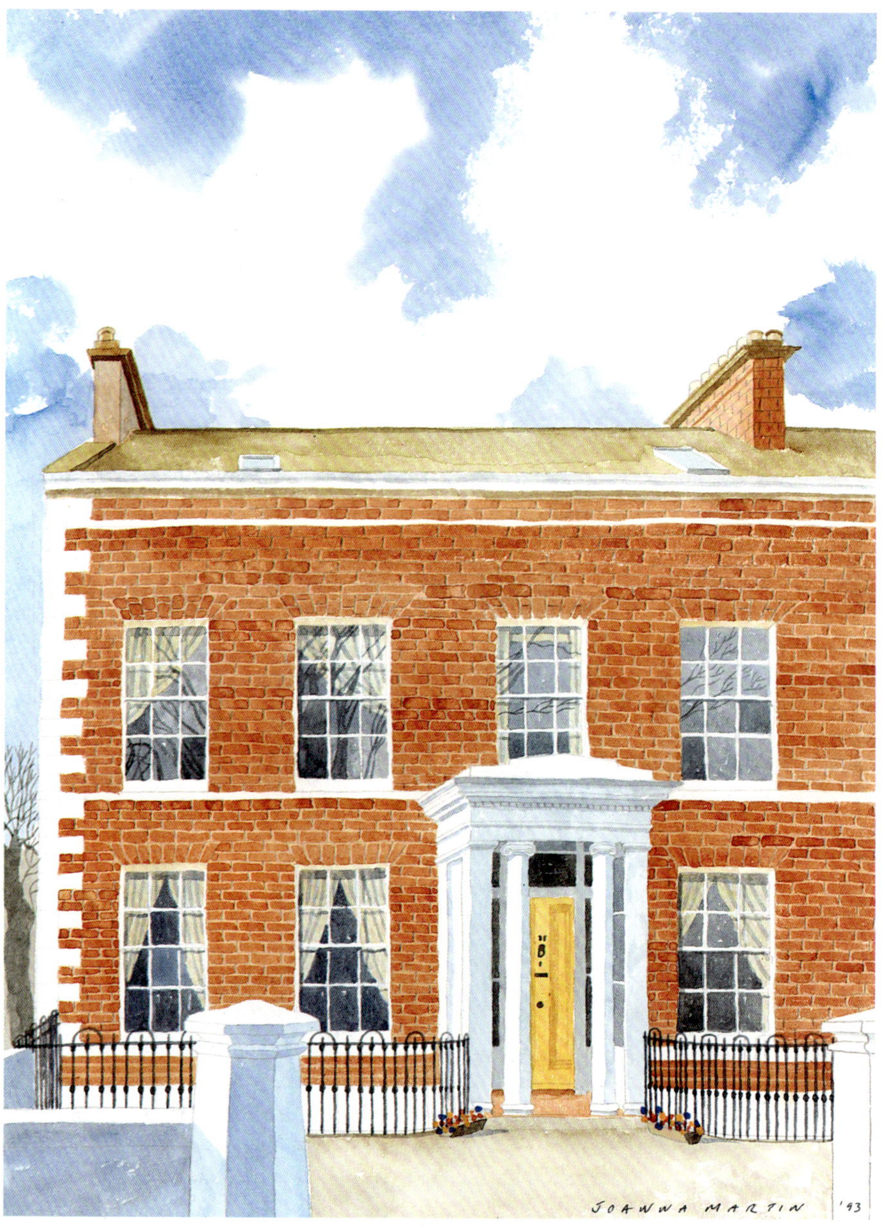
JOANNA MARTIN '93

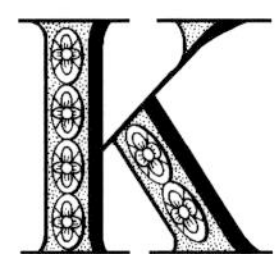

| *Name and Address* | *Telephone* |
| --- | --- |
| | |
| | |
| | |
| | |
| | |
| | |
| | |
| | |
| | |
| | |
| | |
| | |
| | |

## Town House, Victoria Road.

This is one of a pair of rather substantial and handsome semi-detached town houses typical of those which were erected by the mercantile and professional people who moved into the "High Holywood" district. Dating from 1856, they are situated at the corner of Brook Street and occupy a site on high ground immediately overlooking what was once the site of a cornmill that was powered by the river Twisel. This mill was one of three in the immediate neighbourhood built towards the close of the previous century. It was in operation until, following the death of the last owner in 1852, it was pulled down. At the beginning of this century the house next door served as a "dame" school.

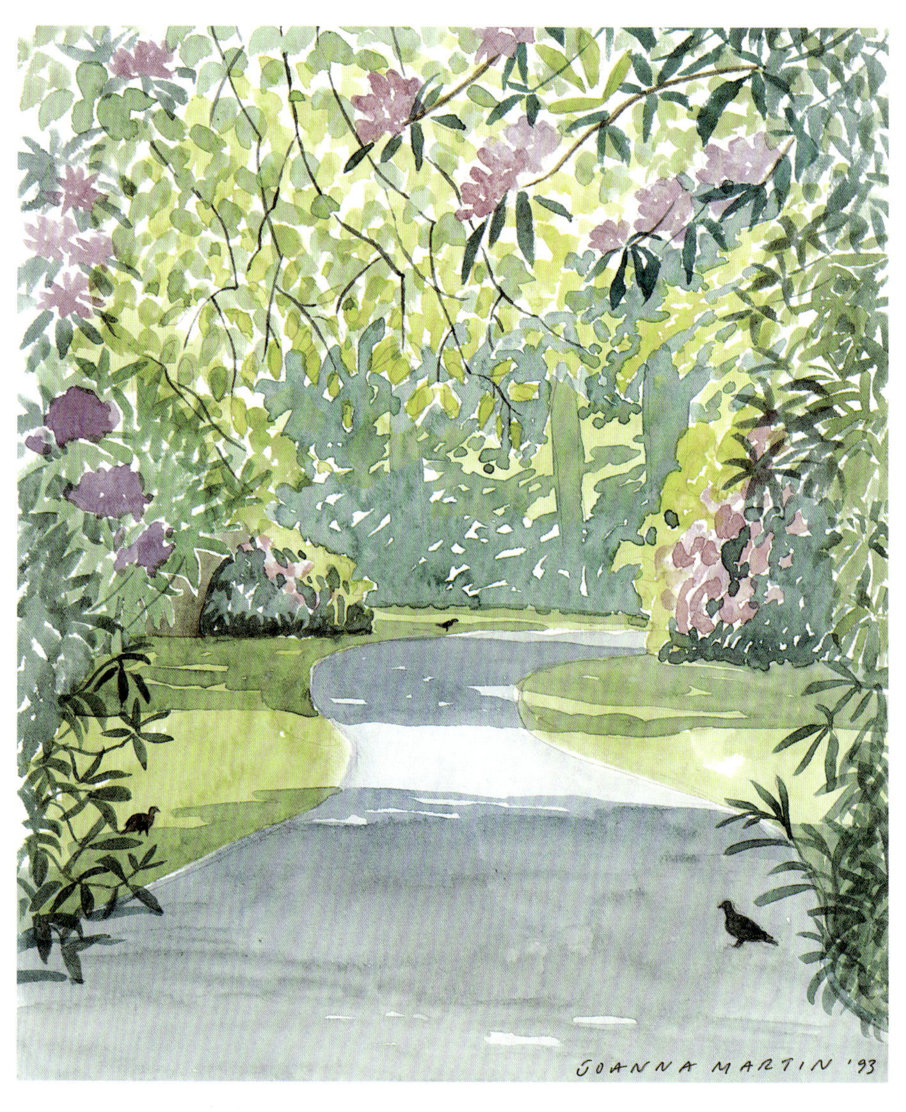
JOANNA MARTIN '93

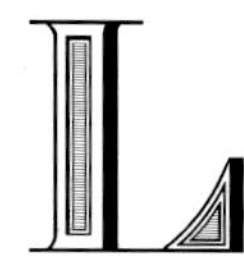

| *Name and Address* | *Telephone* |
| --- | --- |
| | |
| | |
| | |
| | |
| | |
| | |
| | |
| | |
| | |
| | |
| | |
| | |
| | |

**Ballymenoch Park, Bangor Road.**

This extensive park with its mature trees and pleasant paths was laid out shortly after the Second World War in what was the surviving part of the estate surrounding Ballymenoch House. The original mansion, an elegant and almost square structure, was probably built by the Hamilton family in about 1780. It was owned for much of the nineteenth century by the Greg family, successful Belfast merchants. In 1889 it was bought by Sir Daniel Dixon, the first Lord Mayor of Belfast and was burnt down in 1913, allegedly by suffragettes. Its successor, a somewhat less distinguished house, was built by Sir Samuel Kelly the shipping magnate and is now the Eventide Home for the elderly.

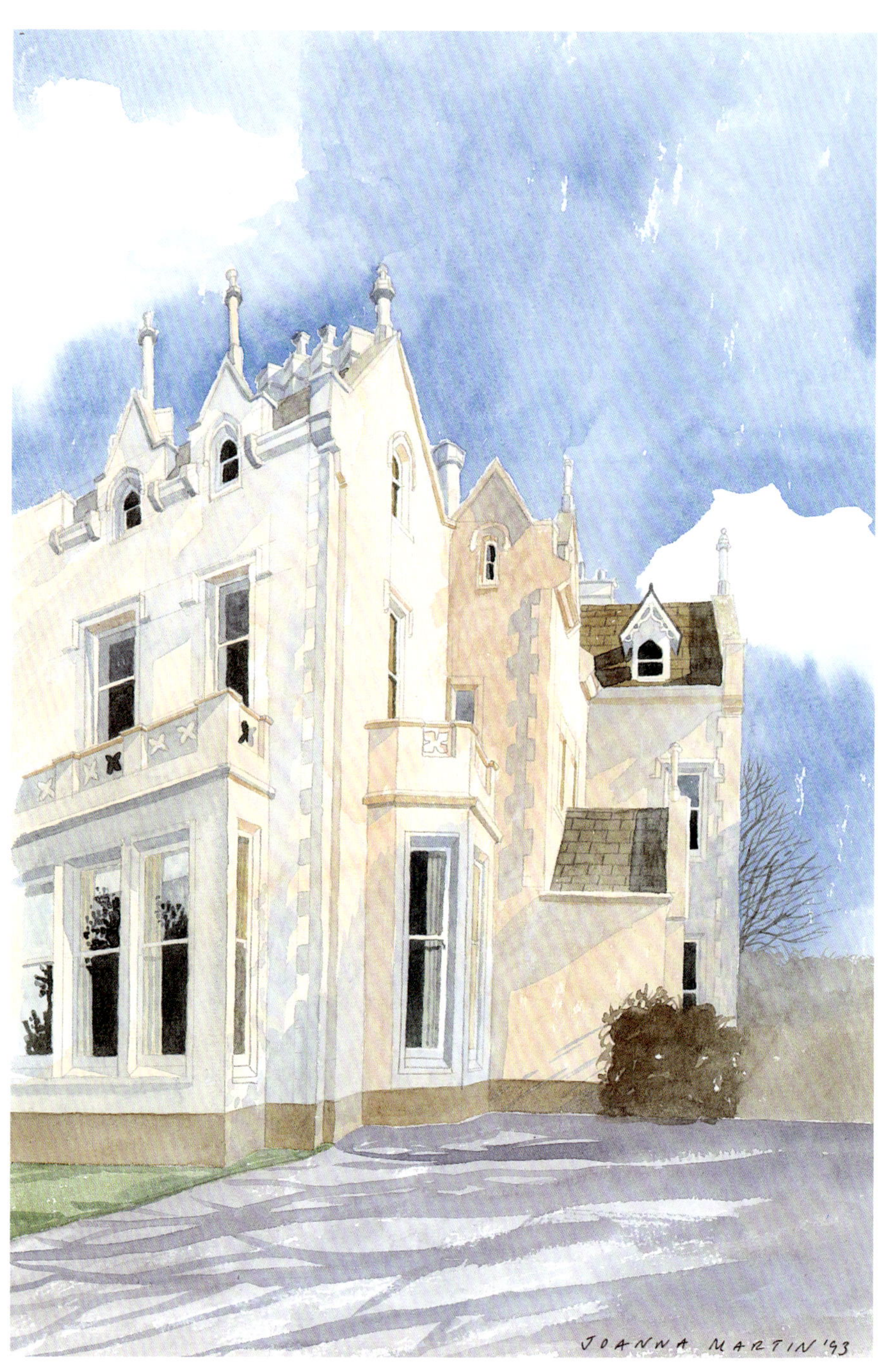
JOANNA MARTIN '93

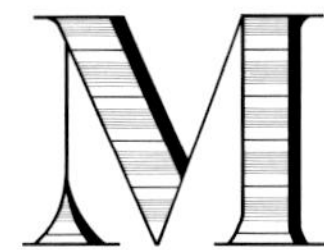

| *Name and Address* | *Telephone* |
|---|---|
| | |
| | |
| | |
| | |
| | |
| | |
| | |
| | |
| | |
| | |
| | |
| | |
| | |

MERCHANTS VILLA, TUDOR PARK.

This impressive neo-Elizabethan pile, originally Tudor Hall, is one of two pairs of semi-detached mansions located on high ground overlooking the Bangor Rd with wooded surroundings. Built in 1849 by Henry Murney, the prosperous tobacco merchant, for a total cost of £6,000, they are good examples of the villas being erected by merchants settling in the area known as "High Holywood" in mid-Victorian times. Rich in detail, these stuccoed houses boast such treatments as drip stones over doors and windows, shouldered gables, ornamental finials and massive lozenge shaped chimney stacks. In the early 1970's most of the grounds were covered by a private housing development.

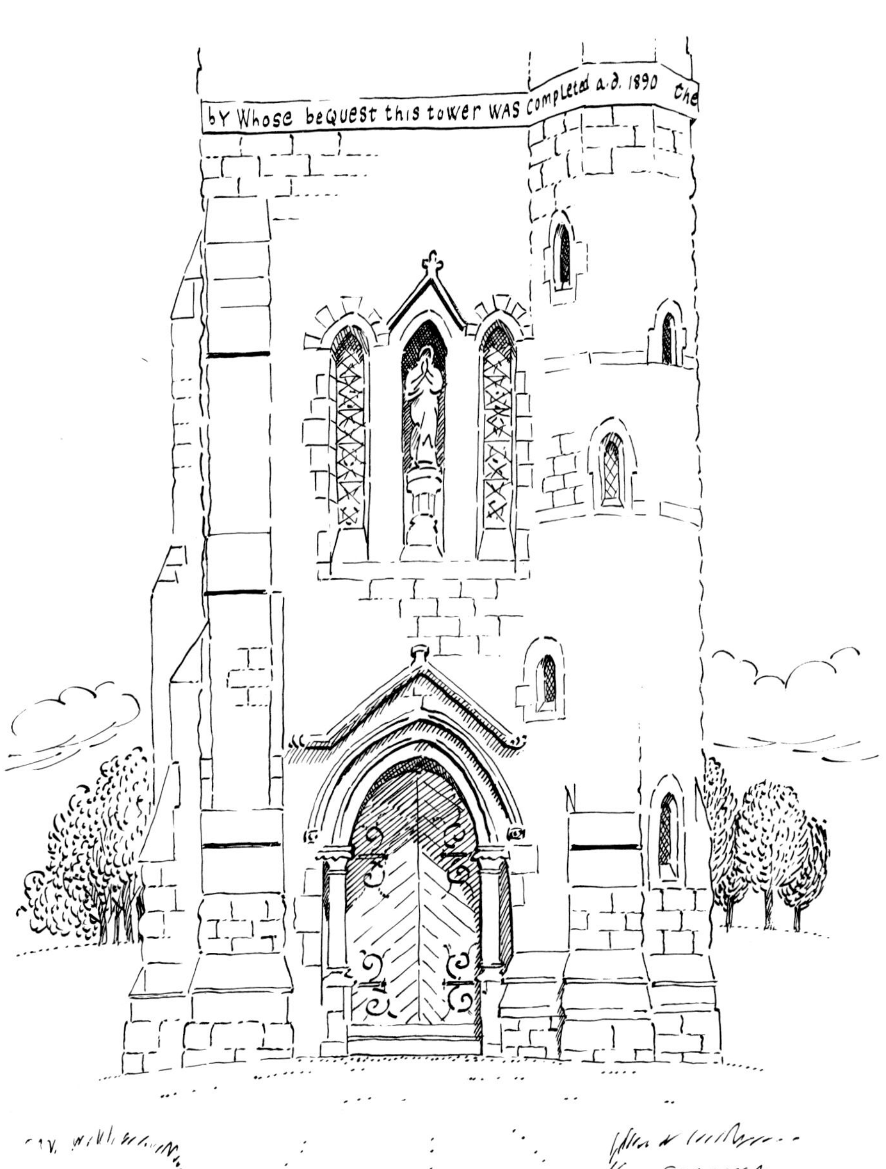
by whose bequest this tower was completed a.d. 1890 the
JOANNA MARTIN '93

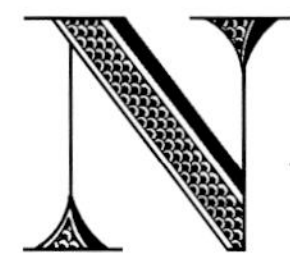

| *Name and Address* | *Telephone* |
|---|---|
| | |
| | |
| | |
| | |
| | |
| | |
| | |
| | |
| | |
| | |
| | |
| | |
| | |

## St. Colmcille's Church.

The first post-Reformation Catholic church in Holywood was St. Patrick's in Church View, consecrated in 1830. To meet the growth in the congregation Timothy Hevey was commissioned by Monsignor O'Laverty, the parish priest, to design a much larger church on a prominent site overlooking the road into Belfast. This was in a most beautiful French Gothic style, and consisted of a nave and chancel with a lofty tower to one side, which was consecrated in 1874. The spire was added in 1891. Sadly the church was totally destroyed by fire in August 1989 although the tower survived. Work has started on a new circular church and the belfry tower, of which the door is illustrated, is to be retained.

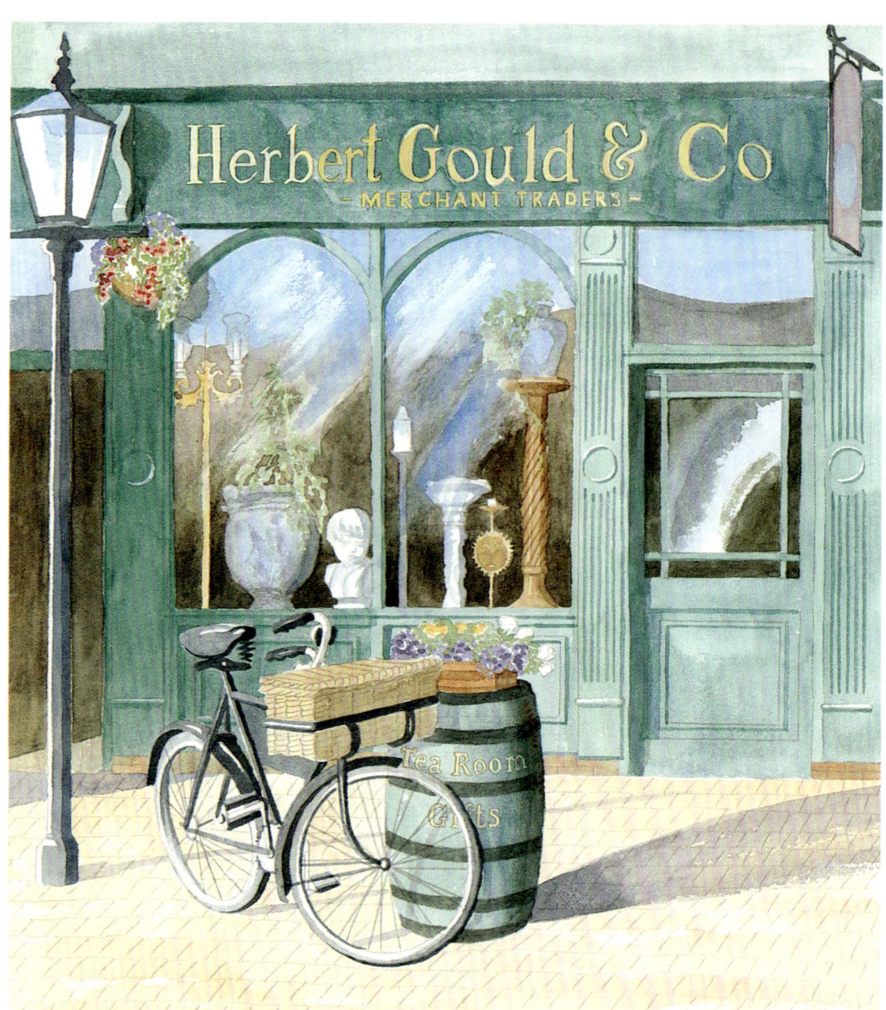
Herbert Gould & Co
- MERCHANT TRADERS -
Tea Room
Gifts
JOANNA MARTIN '93

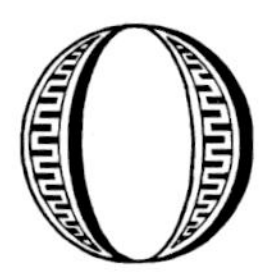

| *Name and Address* | *Telephone* |
|---|---|
| | |
| | |
| | |
| | |
| | |
| | |
| | |
| | |
| | |
| | |
| | |
| | |
| | |

## HERBERT GOULD & CO, CHURCH RD.

This business traces its lineage back to the firm of C.H. Gould & Co. – Merchant Traders which was established in 1897 in Trillick, Co Tyrone selling provisions, tools, drapery etc. The present day company moved to Holywood in 1989 under the auspices of Stephen Gould, the grandson of the original proprietor, and specialises in a range of high quality gifts. Externally the shop's most striking feature is its replica Victorian shopfront which is in sharp contrast to the four storey modern apartment block in which it is situated. This was also completed in 1989 and is called O'Neill's Place as a reminder of the little mid-Victorian court of that name which had previously occupied the site.

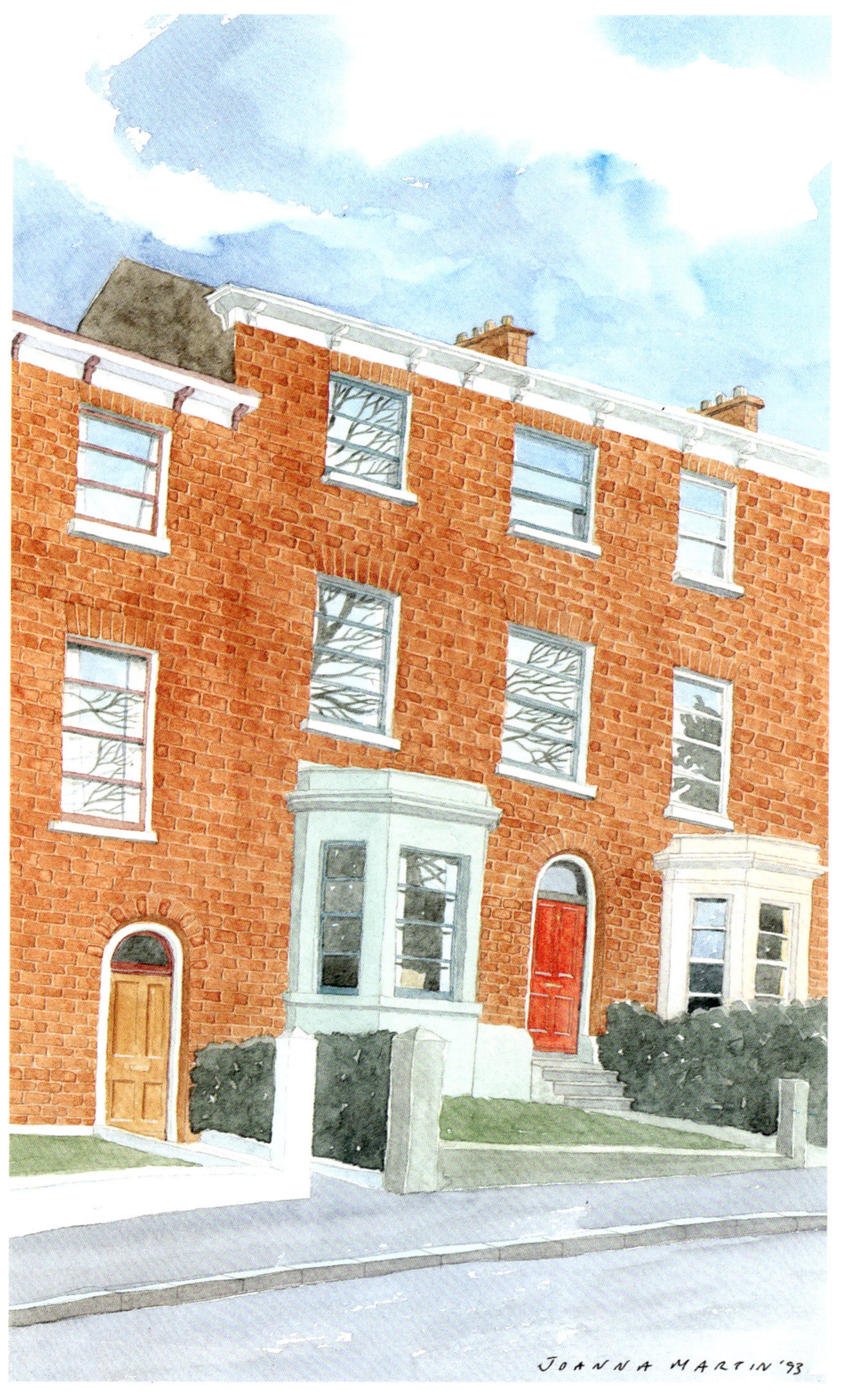
JOANNA MARTIN '93

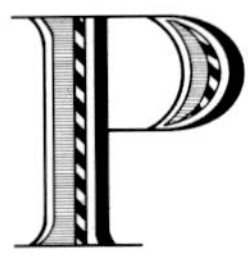

| *Name and Address* | *Telephone* |
|---|---|
| | |
| | |
| | |
| | |
| | |
| | |
| | |
| | |
| | |
| | |
| | |
| | |
| | |

## CHURCHILL TERRACE, CHURCH RD.

This rather fine terrace of nine houses situated directly opposite the Church of Ireland was completed in 1868 by John Browne, a speculative builder from Belfast. Initially they were rented to professional people and the smaller merchants who sought temporary accommodation before perhaps buying somewhat larger dwellings. No 104, in the centre of the illustration, was the home of the distinguished sculptor, Morris Harding M.A. R.H.A from 1925 until his death in 1964 at the age of almost 90. A specialist in animal studies, he was responsible for most of the capitals of the pillars in the nave and the groups of figures on the west front of St. Anne's Cathedral, Belfast.

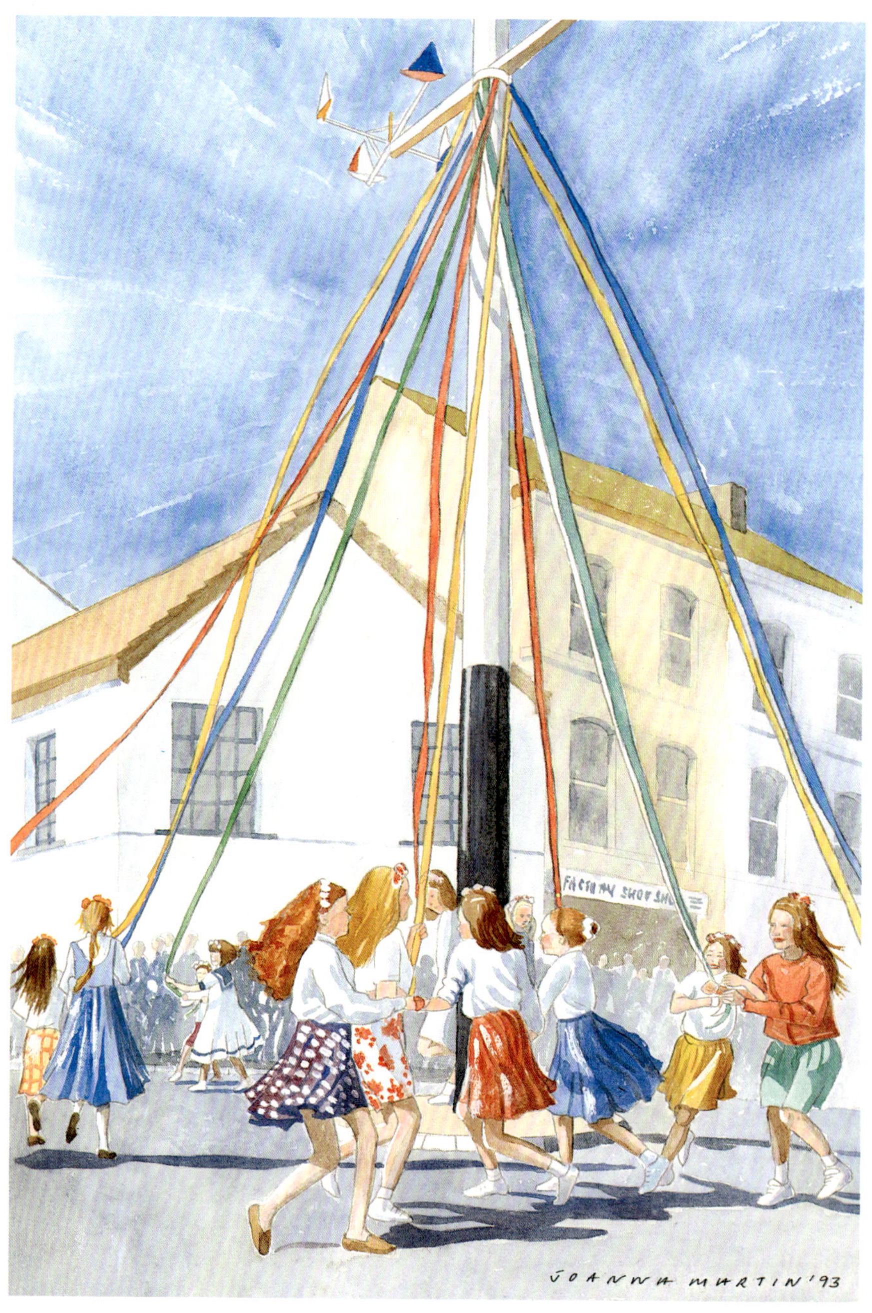
JOANNA MARTIN '93

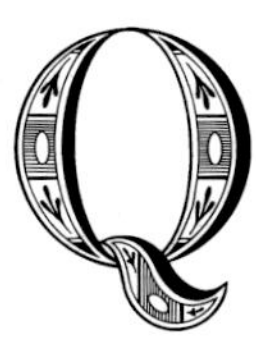

| *Name and Address* | *Telephone* |
|---|---|
| | |
| | |
| | |
| | |
| | |
| | |
| | |
| | |
| | |
| | |
| | |
| | |
| | |

**Maypole.**

For many people the maypole is the most distinguishing feature of Holywood and is nowadays the only one surviving in Ireland. There has been a maypole on or near its present siting at the junction of Shore Rd with High St since about 1620. Like all true maypoles, the early ones at Holywood were no more than about twenty feet tall but, since the the mid nineteenth century they have tended to be three or four times as tall. Made of wood, they tend to rot at the base and they have to be replaced periodically, usually as a gift from a prominent local person. Since 1983 the age-old festivities of dancing around the maypole on Mayday have been revived annually.

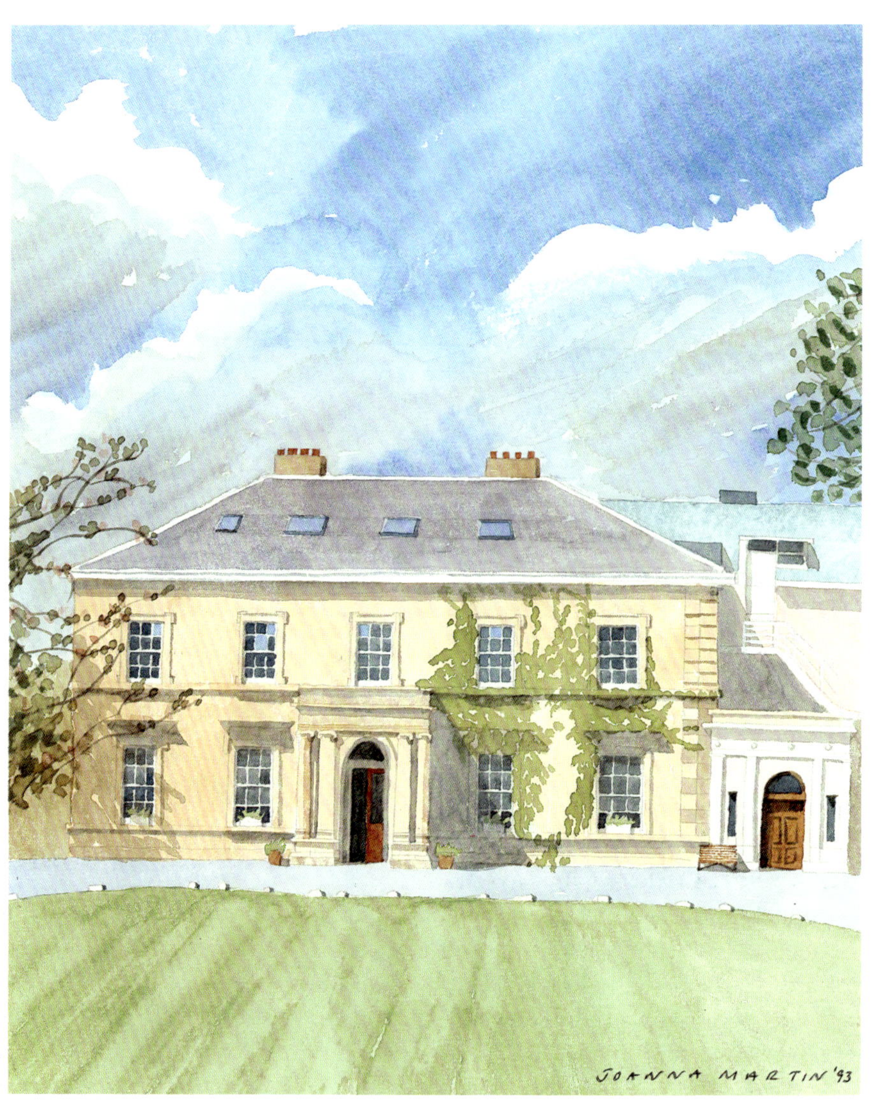
JOANNA MARTIN '93

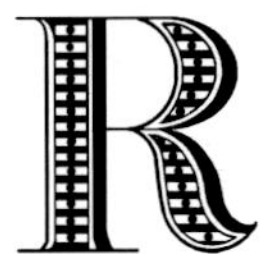

| *Name and Address* | *Telephone* |
|---|---|
| | |
| | |
| | |
| | |
| | |
| | |
| | |
| | |
| | |
| | |
| | |
| | |
| | |

## ROCKPORT SCHOOL, CRAIGAVAD.

Among the large mansions built in spacious grounds carved out of the Kennedy estate was Rockport House erected on a prime coastal site looking towards Carrickfergus in about 1800 by John Turnly, a brewer from Belfast. It remained a private dwelling until the arrival in 1906 of Geoffrey Bing who opened Ulster's first preparatory school in it. Starting out with just five boys, it now has nearly two hundred pupils of both sexes and a most comprehensive curriculum is offered. The school has been repeatedly extended over the years, but happily the original building retains much of its character.

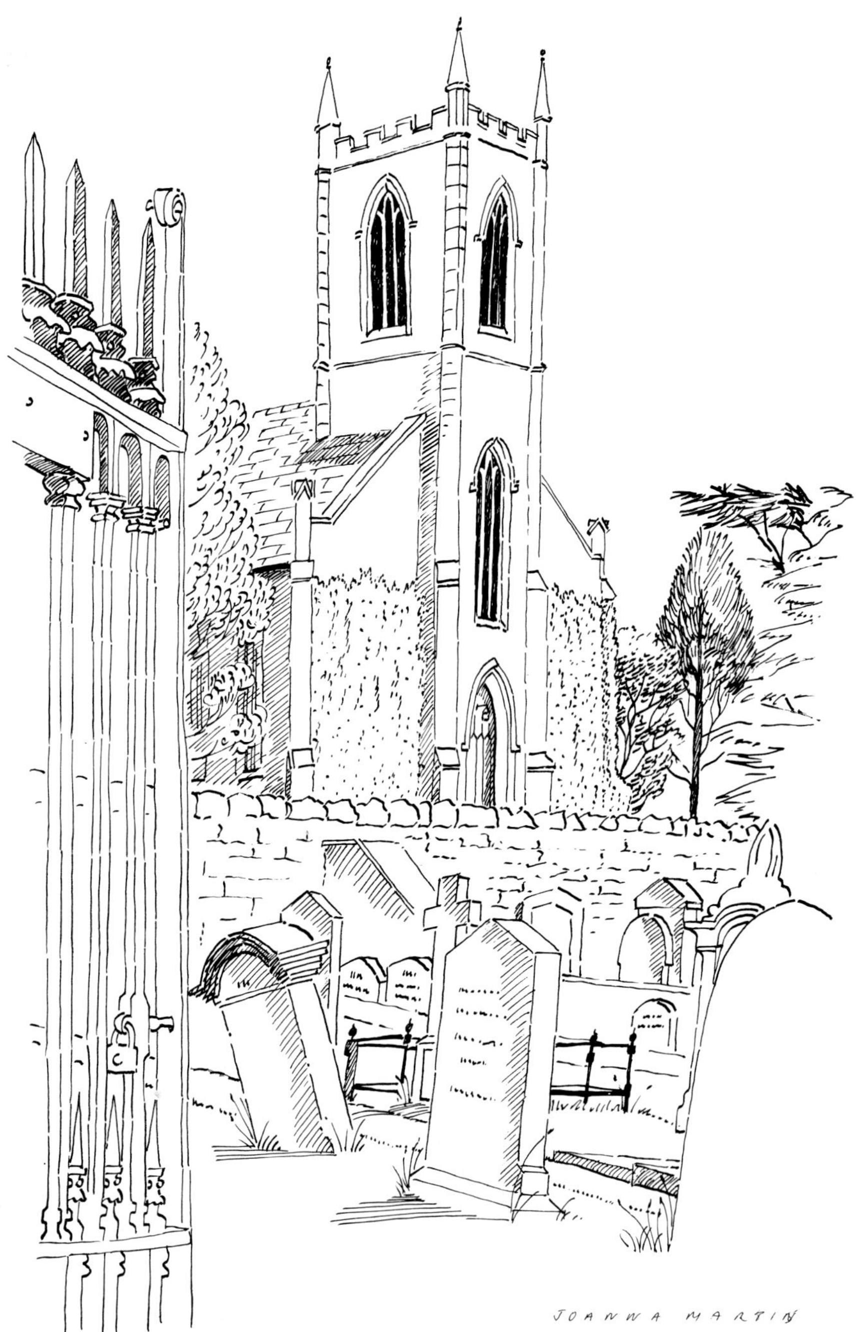
JOANNA MARTIN

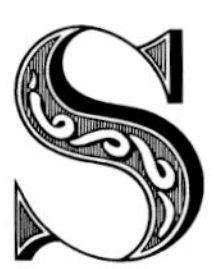

| *Name and Address* | *Telephone* |
|---|---|
| | |
| | |
| | |
| | |
| | |
| | |
| | |
| | |
| | |
| | |
| | |
| | |
| | |

**BANGOR ROAD PRESBYTERIAN CHURCH.**

When the Presbyterians ceased to worship at the Old Priory Church in 1661, they built a meeting house at the bottom of Shore St and remained there until 1726. At that date the congregation was split over the controversy surrounding the Westminster Confession of Faith. Those who subscribed to it moved to Gospel Lane (later Strand St) and in 1841, by which time the congregation had grown substantially, they opened their present church. Designed by their minister, the Rev. William Blackwood in the Gothic Revival style, its frontal appearance echoes that of the nearby old Priory church. The total cost at the time was £1,500.

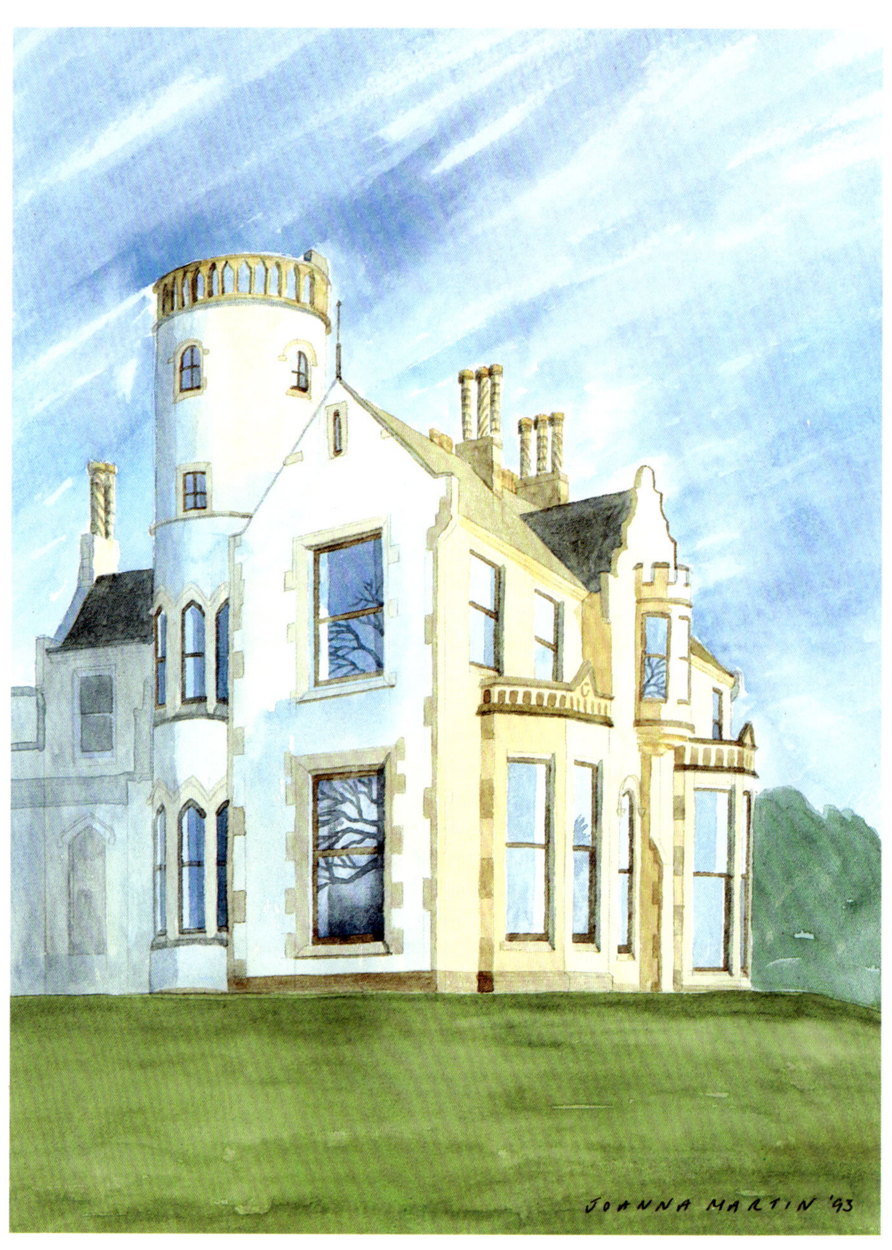
JOANNA MARTIN '93

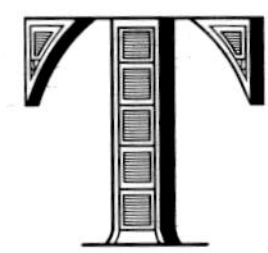

| *Name and Address* | *Telephone* |
|---|---|
| | |
| | |
| | |
| | |
| | |
| | |
| | |
| | |
| | |
| | |
| | |
| | |
| | |

**LORNE, CRAIGAVAD.**

Lorne, on Station Rd, is a rambling mansion built in an attractive mixture of Elizabethan and Jacobean styles of architecture with superb views across spacious grounds towards the Country Antrim hills. It is one of the earliest houses to be built entirely of yellow brick and particularly striking is the wealth of detail on the chimneys and the interior plasterwork. It was erected in the mid 1860's by Henry James Campbell, a retired flax spinner. On his death in1889, Campbell, a bachelor, left Lorne and his entire estate of £200,000 for the purpose of founding a school. Campbell College, Belfast, was the result. In 1945 Lorne became the headquarters of the Girl Guides Association in Northern Ireland.

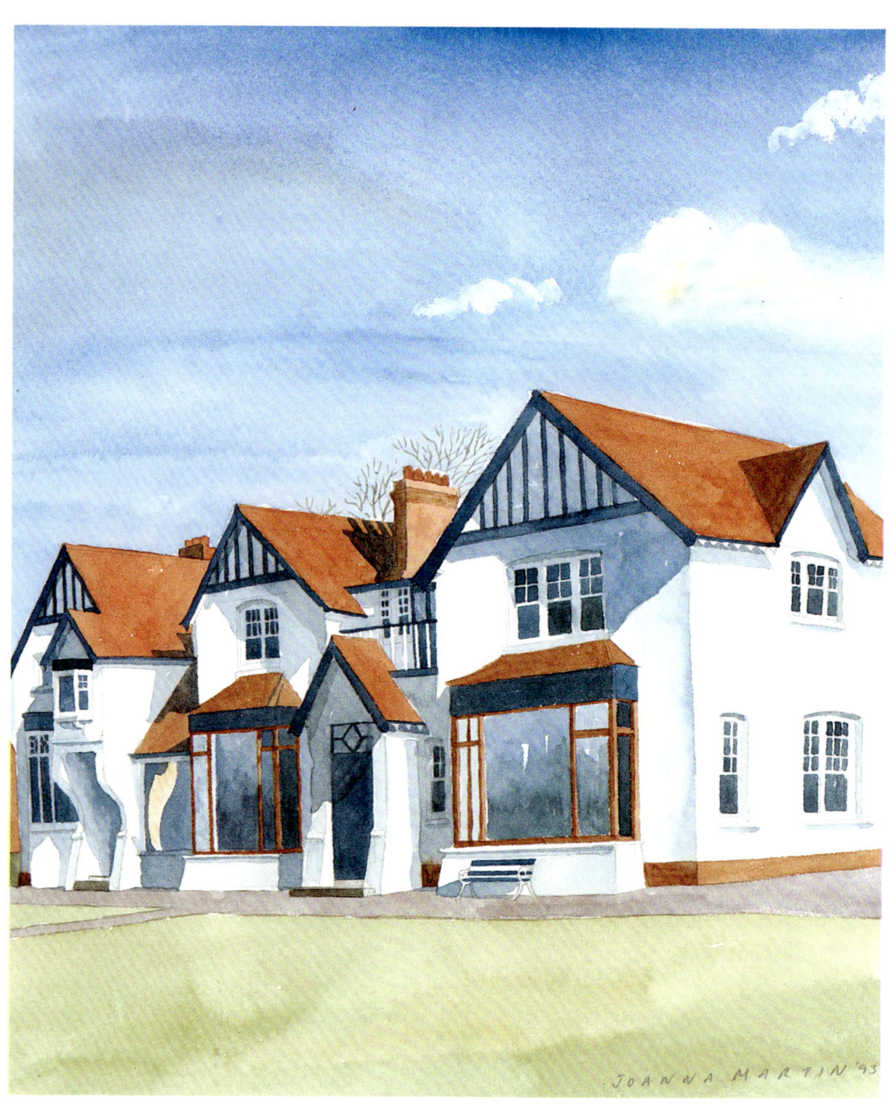
JOANNA MARTIN '93

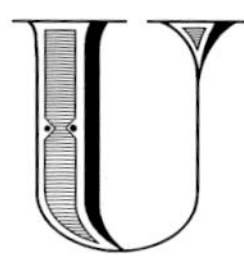

| *Name and Address* | *Telephone* |
| --- | --- |
| | |
| | |
| | |
| | |
| | |
| | |
| | |
| | |
| | |
| | |
| | |
| | |
| | |

**ROYAL NORTH OF IRELAND YACHT CLUB, CULTRA.**

In 1889 the Ulster Canoe Club came into being, and used the old pier and a boat shed that had once belonged to fisherman. The Yacht Club developed from this by 1899 and between 1897 and 1902 the club house was constructed in three stages. Designed by Hartley Patterson, an exponent of the Arts and Crafts movement in Ulster, the building successfully blends architectural features from several different previous ages. Among the club's better known commodores were members of the Workman family who were partners in the ship building firm of Workman and Clark.

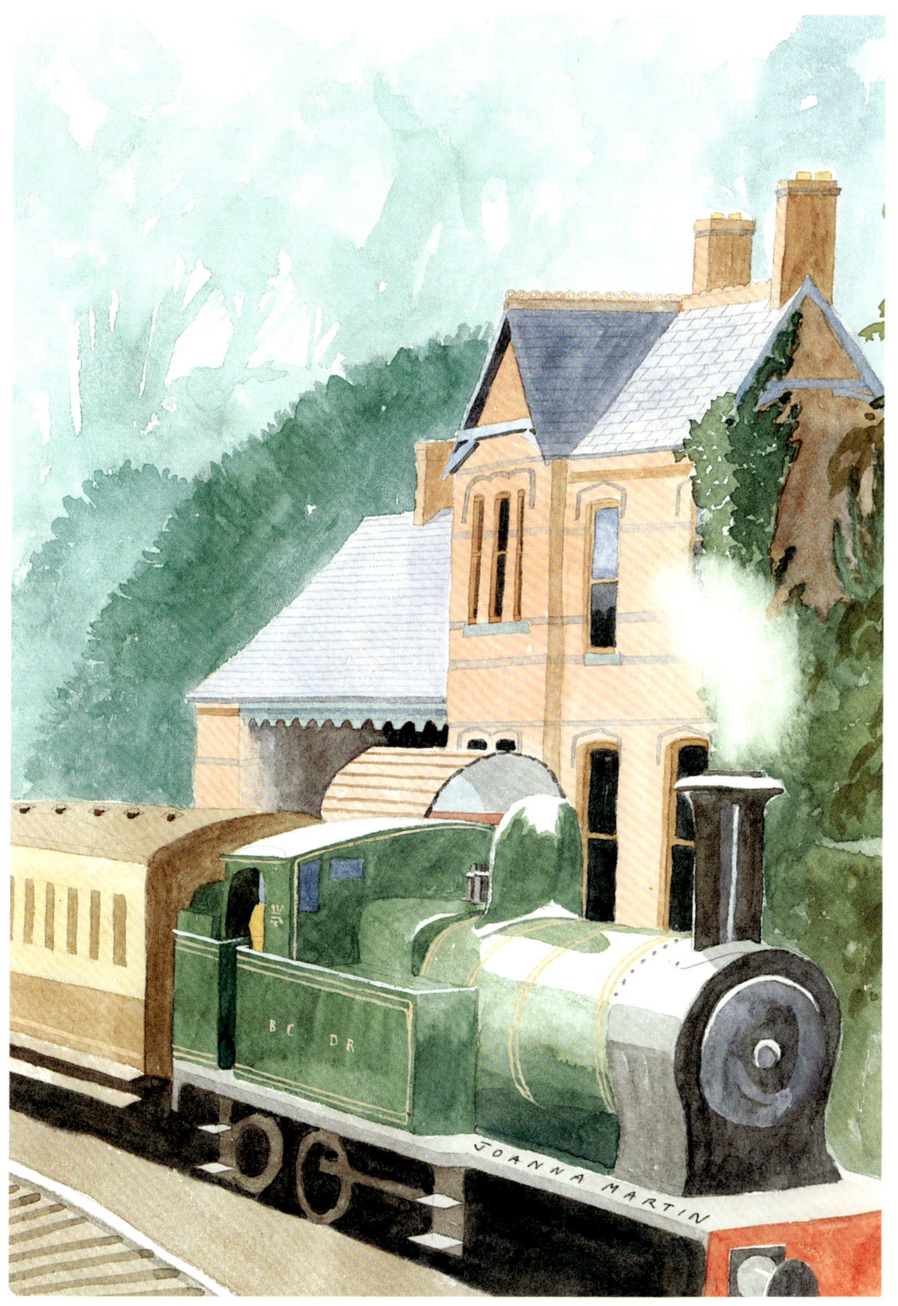
BC DR
JOANNA MARTIN

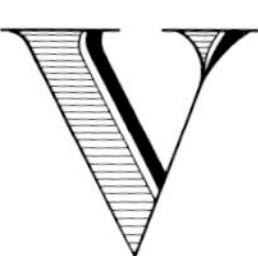

| *Name and Address* | *Telephone* |
| --- | --- |
| | |
| | |
| | |
| | |
| | |
| | |
| | |
| | |
| | |
| | |
| | |
| | |
| | |

## Cultra Railway Station

When the Belfast and County Down Railway Company extended their Belfast to Holywood railway line to Bangor between 1859 and 1865, the work necessitated both the construction of embankments and cuttings, as well as the provision of new station buildings. These were all different and were designed by Charles Lanyon, the noted architect who was also the railway company's chief engineer. This one at Cultra, sited on the "down" platform is an attractive composition in red brick and incorporates both the station master's house, ticket office and waiting room. The picture shows an impression of one of the B.&C.D.R trains (now at the transport museum) in the station.

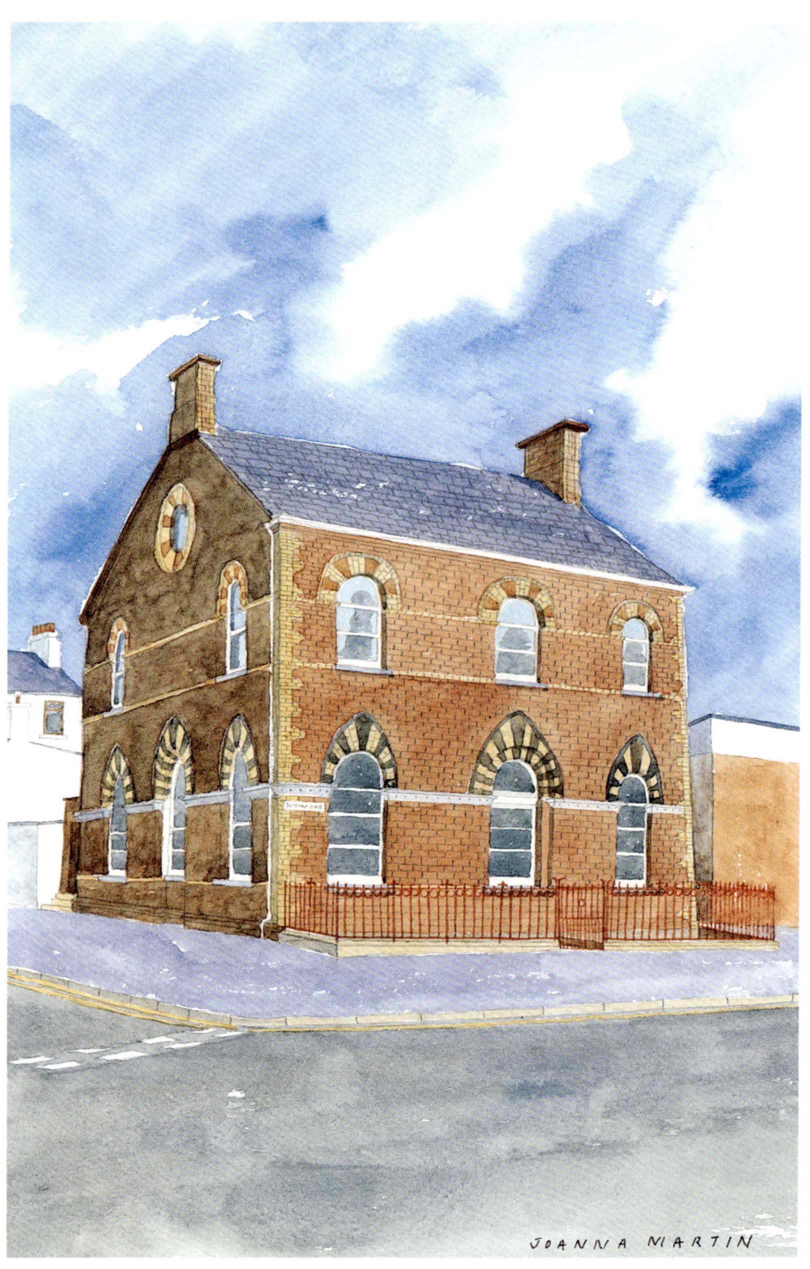
JOANNA MARTIN

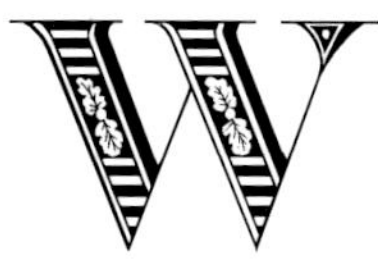

| *Name and Address* | *Telephone* |
|---|---|
| | |
| | |
| | |
| | |
| | |
| | |
| | |
| | |
| | |
| | |
| | |
| | |
| | |

**ORANGE HALL, SULLIVAN PLACE.**

This building was promoted by the Holywood Royal Standard (L.O.L 1906) which, since its foundation in 1868 until the opening of the new hall, had met in what is now the Heasley Hall in Church View. The hall was built between 1879 and 1882 to designs by William Batt, a distinguishing characteristic being the extensive use of polychrome brick. The treatment to the door and window heads suggests Lombardic influence. Overall, the building is representative of public architecture at that period. The central window facing Sullivan Place was originally a door. Part of the building is currently used by the Department of Health and Social Services.

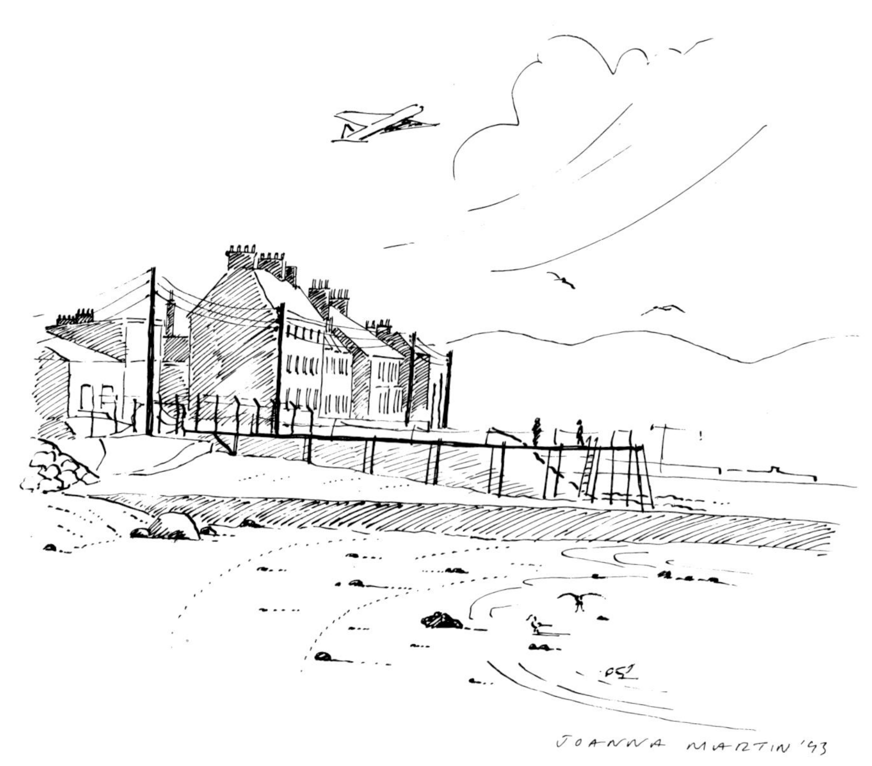
JOANNA MARTIN '93

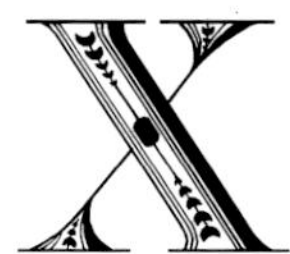

| *Name and Address* | *Telephone* |
|---|---|
| | |
| | |
| | |
| | |
| | |
| | |
| | |
| | |
| | |
| | |
| | |
| | |
| | |

## THE KINNEGAR.

This area was, until the 1850's, a spit of desolate rough pasture and sand dunes surrounded on three sides by the sea and, as such, was always separate from Holywood. It was frequented by people gathering mussels and, in summer, hunting rabbits – the name is derived from the Irish for rabbit warren. Housing appeared between 1858 and 1900 on the part nearer Holywood, whilst in the 1880's the dunes were the venue for the Belfast Golf Club, the local cricket club and military camps. The picture which is looking westward from the Esplanade, itself dating from the 1860's, shows on the right the pier belonging to Holywood Yacht Club and a mile or so beyond is Belfast City Airport which opened in 1982.

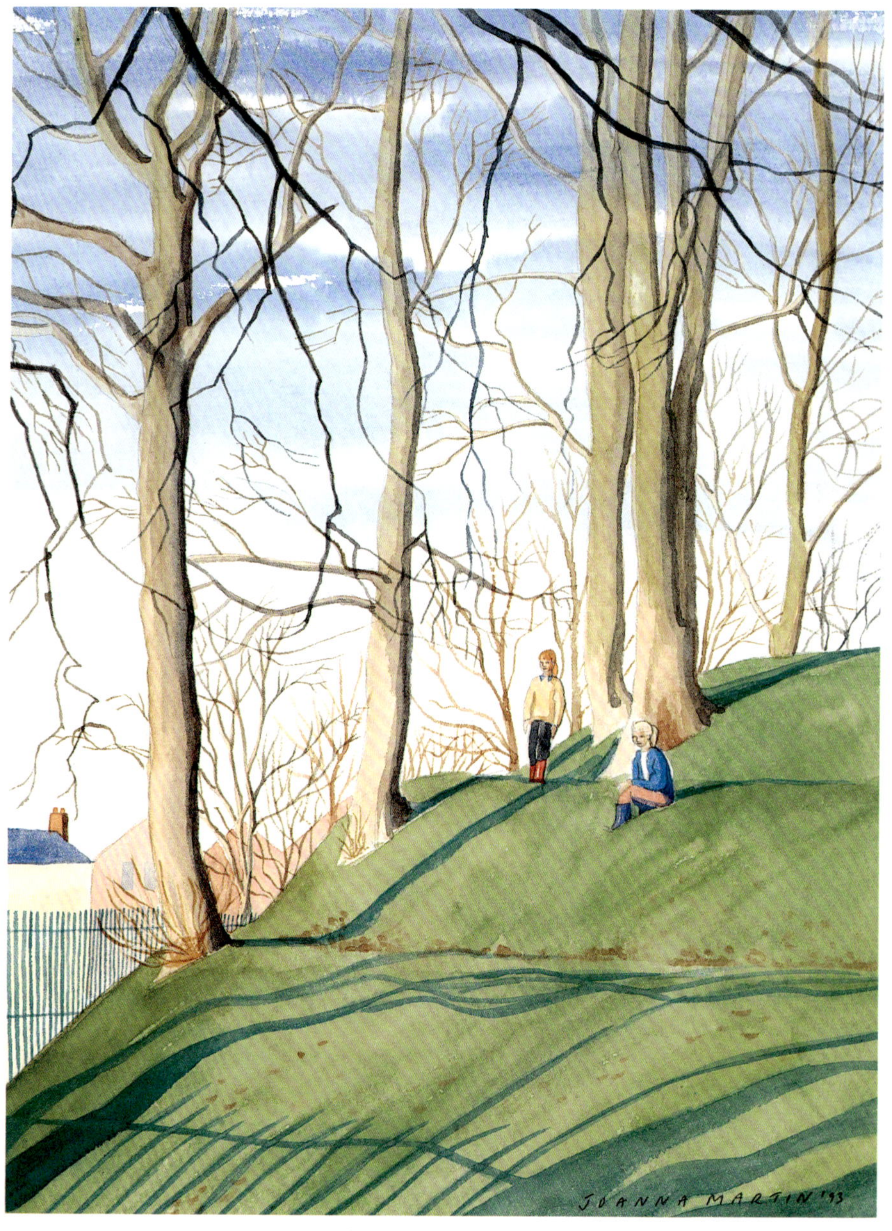
JOANNA MARTIN '93

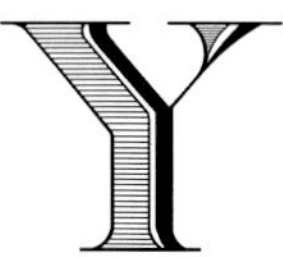

| *Name and Address* | *Telephone* |
| --- | --- |
| | |
| | |
| | |
| | |
| | |
| | |
| | |
| | |
| | |
| | |
| | |
| | |
| | |

## Holywood Motte.

This is one in a chain of defensive forts stretching from Donaghadee to Ballyderry, erected by the Anglo–Norman settlers in the late 12th century in order to subdue the native Irish as they strove to conquer Ulster. An artificially raised conical mound of earth, topped by a stout timber palisade with a small timber castle in the centre, it was highly effective both as a look out and as a place of defence. King John, during his invasion of Ulster, spent one night here in July 1210 before proceeding along the military road to the motte at Dundonald. Located in a quiet part of the town near Brook St, it is heavily wooded and stands in a small park.

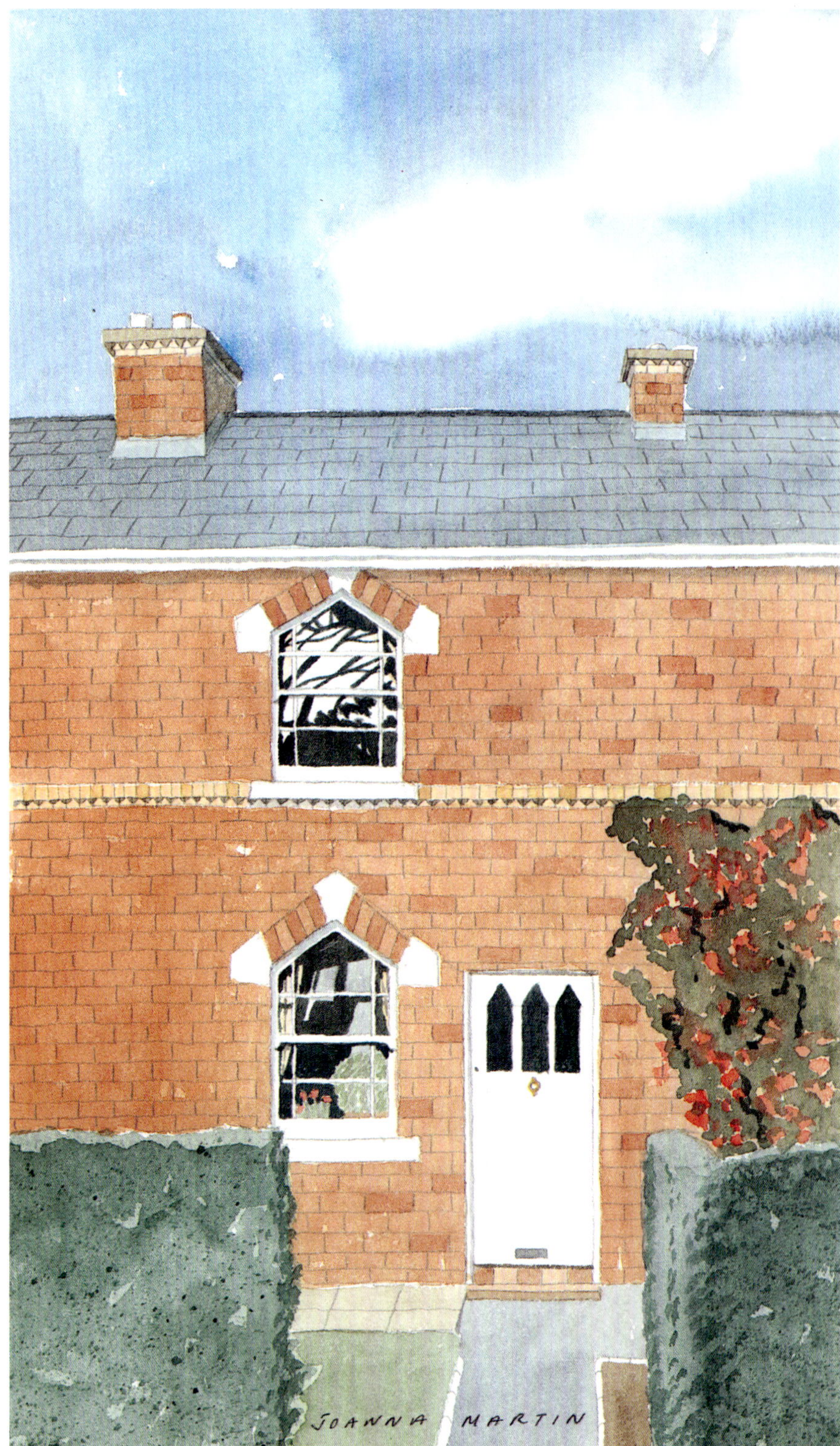
JOANNA MARTIN

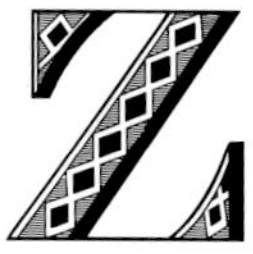

| *Name and Address* | *Telephone* |
|---|---|
| | |
| | |
| | |
| | |
| | |
| | |
| | |
| | |
| | |
| | |
| | |
| | |
| | |

## Coastguard Cottages, Farmhill Road.

In the late 1870's new coastguard stations were erected around the coast of Ireland to several different standard designs. This particular group consists of a tower type dwelling and a large house with a half hip roof linked by a row of two storey cottages. The entire group is built of red brick and is distinguished by such features as yellow brick banding in dog-tooth pattern and triangular-headed windows. Curiously, for coastguard cottages, this group is located nearly half a mile inland, its view over the lough has always been obscured by trees and it is at right angles to the coast!

# *Local Business and Service Directory*

Although Holywood is primarily a dormitory town it has a thriving business heart serving both the local people and the wider community.

We would like to thank the following businesses whose enthusiasm and support has made this celebration of Holywood possible.

*Unless otherwise stated all businesses listed are in Holywood (STD code 0232)*

| | | Tel | Fax |
|---|---|---|---|
| Art Gallery and Book Binding | | | |
| PRIORY ART GALLERY | 10 SHORE RD | 428173 | |
| Beauty Salon | | | |
| DEDORAH NEILL HEALTH AND BEAUTY CLINIC | KING HOUSE, 39–41 HIGH ST | 424999 | |
| Carpets, Vinyls and Rugs | | | |
| HOLYWOOD CARPET CENTRE | 127 HIGH ST | 428157 | |
| Chartered Accountant | | | |
| CAROLINE ANDERSON | 50 HIGH ST | 422618 | 423444 |
| Chartered Architect | | | |
| GORDON MCKNIGHT PARTNERSHIP | 31 SHORE RD | 426888 | 427047 |
| Chemist | | | |
| SWEENEY'S PHARMACY | 52 HIGH ST | 422222 | 654054 |
| Delicatessen | | | |
| PANINI | 25 CHURCH RD | 427774 | 427774 |
| Dental Surgery | | | |
| ERIC HEYES B.D.S | 128 HIGH ST | 423306 | |
| Electrical Contractors | | | |
| KENNEDY ENGINEERING SERVICES | UNIT 2 KING HOUSE, 39–41 HIGH ST | 425921 | 425921 |
| Estate Agents, Residential | | | |
| THE ERIC CAIRNS PARTNERSHIP | 60A HIGH ST | 428989 | 428844 |
| | 151 STRANMILLIS RD | 668888 | 683330 |
| Florist | | | |
| THE FLOWERSHOP | UNIT 4 SULLIVAN PL. | 427372 | |
| Footwear Distributor | | | |
| STAFFORD & MITCHELL (N.I) LTD | 35 HIBERNIA ST | 424890 | 428242 |

| | | Tel | Fax |
|---|---|---|---|
| Gift Shop and Tea Room | | | |
| HERBERT GOULD & CO | 21–23 CHURCH RD | 427916 /428589 | 428396 |
| Graphic Designer/Illustrator | | | |
| JOANNA MARTIN, THE ATTIC STUDIO, 22 SHORE RD | | 426728/427861 | |
| Guesthouse | | | |
| RAYANNE GUESTHOUSE | 60 DEMESNE RD | 425859 | 425859 |
| Kitchens,Bathrooms and Bedrooms | | | |
| THOMAS DESIGN | 129 HIGH ST | 428842 | 428842 |
| Outdoor Clothing and Equipment | | | |
| EXTREMES OUTDOORS | 49 HIGH ST | 428529 | 428529 |
| Paint, Wallpaper Fabrics | | | |
| HOLYWOOD HOME DECOR LTD | 2–4 CHURCH RD | 428347 | |
| Photography | | | |
| JEREMY ROWEL FRIERS PHOTOGRAPHY | MILLBANK HOUSE, 33 VICTORIA RD | 423939/ 0850 400273 | |
| PR Consultancy | | | |
| IPR CONSULTANTS LTD | THE COMMUNICATIONS CENTRE, 27 SHORE RD | 425412 | 427094 |
| Public House | | | |
| THE BEAR | 62 HIGH ST | 426837/428802 | |
| Restaurant | | | |
| IONA BISTRO | 27 CHURCH RD | 425655 | |
| LE RESTAURANT SANTÉ | 30 HIGH ST | 428880 | |
| Surveyors and Valuers | | | |
| BRIAN PATTERSON & CO | 22 SHORE RD | 428292 | 428280 |
| Television Production Company | | | |
| BRIAN WADDELL PRODUCTIONS LTD | CRESCENT HOUSE, 14 HIGH ST | 427646 | 427922 |
| Wholefoods, Herbal Medicines | | | |
| IONA SHOP | 27 CHURCH RD | 428597 | |
| Wholesale Rope and Twine | | | |
| STEVE ORR LTD | P.O BOX 5, HOLYWOOD | 428000 | 428153 |

# *Local Public Service Directory*

| | Tel |
|---|---|
| Cemetery | |
| HOLYWOOD CEMETERY | 424898 |
| Citizens Advice Bureau | |
| HOLYWOOD | 428288 |
| Council | |
| NORTH DOWN BOROUGH COUNCIL | (0247) 270371 |
| Community Centre | |
| QUEENS HALL | 422423 |
| Health Centres | |
| REDBURN HEALTH CLINIC | 423697 |
| HIGH ST | 426881 |
| Heritage Centre | |
| NORTH DOWN HERITAGE CENTRE | (0247) 271200 |
| Police | |
| HOLYWOOD POLICE STATION | 650222 |
| Leisure Centre | |
| BANGOR CASTLE LEISURE CENTRE | (0247) 270271 |
| Library | |
| HOLYWOOD LIBRARY | 424232 |
| Electricity Supply | |
| FAILURE OF SUPPLY | (0247) 461521 |
| Water | |
| DEPT OF ENVIRONMENT WATER SERVICE | 746581 |

# *Open Diary*

This section is provided for recording personal dates such as birthdays, anniversaries and other important annual events.

# January

*1*

*2*

*3*

*4*

*5*

*6*

*7*

*8*

*9*

*10*

*11*

*12*

*13*

*14*

*15*

*16*

*17*

*18*

*19*

*20*

*21*

*22*

*23*

*24*

*25*

*26*

*27*

*28*

*29*

*30*

*31*

# February

*1*

*2*

*3*

*4*

*5*

*6*

*7*

*8*

*9*

*10*

*11*

*12*

*13*

*14*

*15*

*16*

*17*

*18*

*19*

*20*

*21*

*22*

*23*

*24*

*25*

*26*

*27*

*28*

*29*

# March

*1*

*2*

*3*

*4*

*5*

*6*

*7*

*8*

*9*

*10*

*11*

*12*

*13*

*14*

*15*

*16*

*17*

*18*

*19*

*20*

*21*

*22*

*23*

*24*

*25*

*26*

*27*

*28*

*29*

*30*

*31*

# April

*1*

*2*

*3*

*4*

*5*

*6*

*7*

*8*

*9*

*10*

*11*

*12*

*13*

*14*

*15*

*16*

*17*

*18*

*19*

*20*

*21*

*22*

*23*

*24*

*25*

*26*

*27*

*28*

*29*

*30*

# May

*1*

*2*

*3*

*4*

*5*

*6*

*7*

*8*

*9*

*10*

*11*

*12*

*13*

*14*

*15*

*16*

*17*

*18*

*19*

*20*

*21*

*22*

*23*

*24*

*25*

*26*

*27*

*28*

*29*

*30*

*31*

# June

*1*

*2*

*3*

*4*

*5*

*6*

*7*

*8*

*9*

*10*

*11*

*12*

*13*

*14*

*15*

*16*

*17*

*18*

*19*

*20*

*21*

*22*

*23*

*24*

*25*

*26*

*27*

*28*

*29*

*30*

# July

*1*

*2*

*3*

*4*

*5*

*6*

*7*

*8*

*9*

*10*

*11*

*12*

*13*

*14*

*15*

*16*

*17*

*18*

*19*

*20*

*21*

*22*

*23*

*24*

*25*

*26*

*27*

*28*

*29*

*30*

*31*

# August

*1*

*2*

*3*

*4*

*5*

*6*

*7*

*8*

*9*

*10*

*11*

*12*

*13*

*14*

*15*

*16*

*17*

*18*

*19*

*20*

*21*

*22*

*23*

*24*

*25*

*26*

*27*

*28*

*29*

*30*

*31*

# September

*1*

*2*

*3*

*4*

*5*

*6*

*7*

*8*

*9*

*10*

*11*

*12*

*13*

*14*

*15*

*16*

*17*

*18*

*19*

*20*

*21*

*22*

*23*

*24*

*25*

*26*

*27*

*28*

*29*

*30*

# October

*1*

*2*

*3*

*4*

*5*

*6*

*7*

*8*

*9*

*10*

*11*

*12*

*13*

*14*

*15*

*16*

*17*

*18*

*19*

*20*

*21*

*22*

*23*

*24*

*25*

*26*

*27*

*28*

*29*

*30*

*31*

# November

*1*

*2*

*3*

*4*

*5*

*6*

*7*

*8*

*9*

*10*

*11*

*12*

*13*

*14*

*15*

*16*

*17*

*18*

*19*

*20*

*21*

*22*

*23*

*24*

*25*

*26*

*27*

*28*

*29*

*30*

# December

*1*

*2*

*3*

*4*

*5*

*6*

*7*

*8*

*9*

*10*

*11*

*12*

*13*

*14*

*15*

*16*

*17*

*18*

*19*

*20*

*21*

*22*

*23*

*24*

*25*

*26*

*27*

*28*

*29*

*30*

*31*

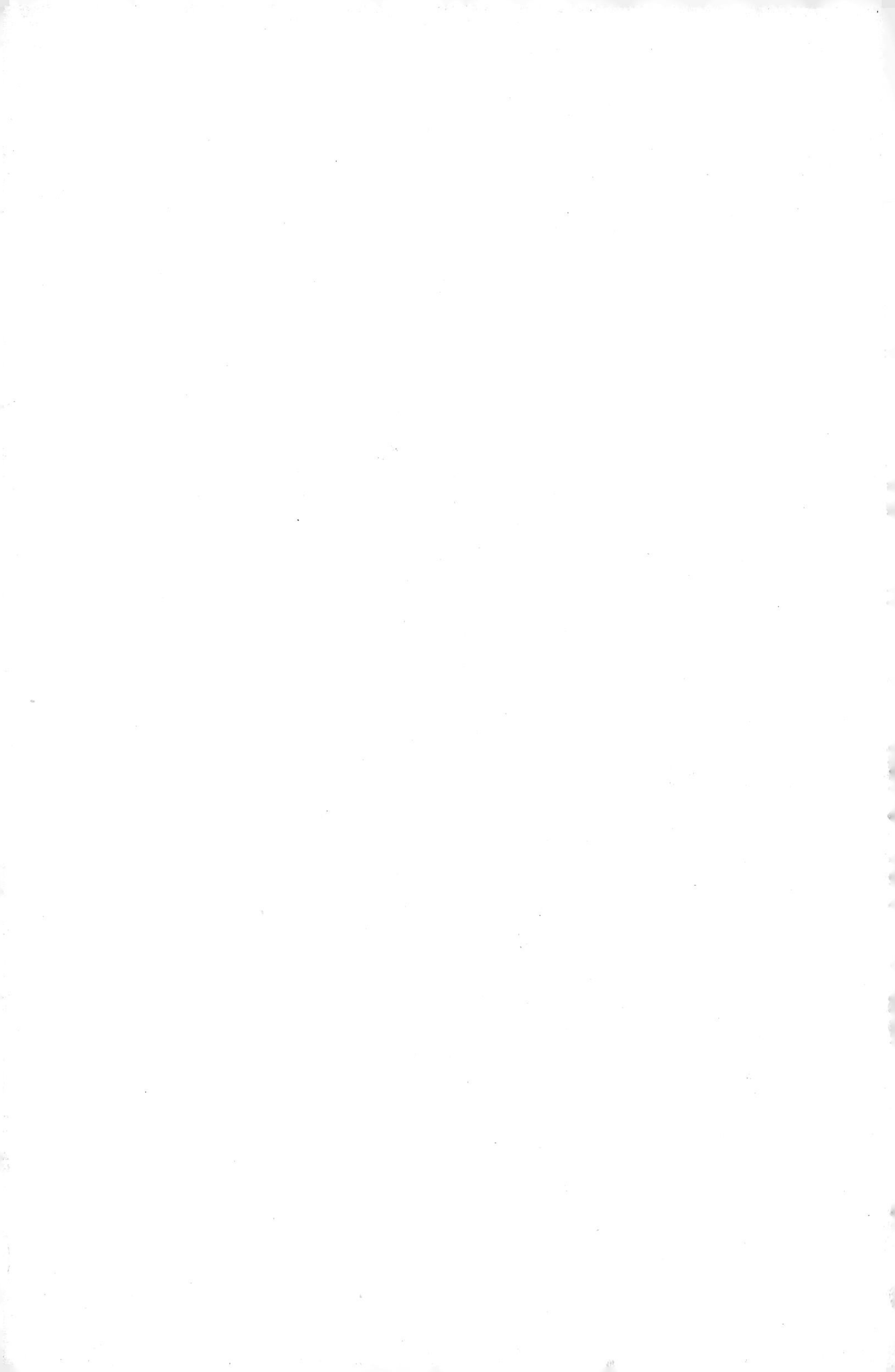